the
big book
of HAPPY

500 GAMES & ACTIVITIES

for ages 2 to 6

Michelle Kennedy

METRO BOOKS
NEW YORK

This book was conceived, designed, and produced by
Ivy Press
The Old Candlemakers
West Street, Lewes,
East Sussex BN7 2NZ, U.K.

Creative Director *Peter Bridgewater*
Publisher *Jason Hook*
Editorial Director *Caroline Earle*
Art Director *Clare Harris*
Designer *Clare Barber*
Illustrations *Ivan Hissey*

Metro Books
122 Fifth Avenue
New York, NY 10011

ISBN-13: 978-1-4351-0544-7
ISBN-10: 1-4351-0544-3

Printed and bound in China

1 3 5 7 9 10 8 6 4 2

Contents

Introduction

Toddlers and preschoolers
are ingenious. Give them a
cardboard box, a couple of
empty plastic bottles, or a bag of fabric and
they can busy themselves for hours...well, hours
if you add them up ten minutes at a time.

I've never liked the idea of being my children's
"entertainer." I don't try to entertain my children—I try
to inspire them to come up with their own ideas. This
book will help you find a variety of ways to inspire your
own children's creativity, desire to learn, or ability to just
"shake out the sillies." Divided
into categories, each section
provides you with games and
activities for almost any
situation—from a long car
ride to a family party.

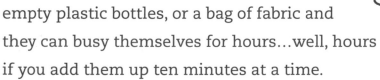

ADULT SUPERVISION

Most activities are made up of things you will find around the house—some require a trip to a store or yard sale and some type of assembly beforehand (but we tried to make 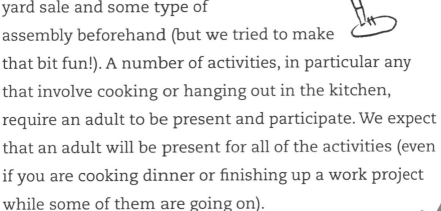 that bit fun!). A number of activities, in particular any that involve cooking or hanging out in the kitchen, require an adult to be present and participate. We expect that an adult will be present for all of the activities (even if you are cooking dinner or finishing up a work project while some of them are going on).

Of course, any activity that calls for the use of scissors, frying, mixing, baking, plugging anything in, or small items like beads require an adult to participate. Have fun...and remember, they are only this little once!

AGE RANGE AND TIMING

Each activity lists four icons to denote an appropriate minimum age, number of players, game time, and amount of equipment needed—see page 10 for a guide to the icons. The activities in this book are aimed at children aged two to six years old, but if you have older children who want to participate—let them—they'll be very helpful. And if you have a child younger than the recommended age, it's up to you to determine if your child is ready for the activity. For some games, it's good to have a time limit. This is the amount of time it should take for you to set up a game and play it with the kids before

they start to get bored or restless. This is also a good way to plan if you need a game for a certain space of time in a scout meeting or party.

INSPIRATION AND LEARNING

Don't think that these are the final word. You can use these activities as inspiration for your own, and elaborate on them. If your toddler found a much better way to use a box than we did, then go with it—don't feel hindered by the instructions! Then please let us know what you did. Many of these activities have other benefits such as development of fine motor skills ("Learning Fun"), we don't list them—the activities are meant to be fun and will, undoubtedly, help your child develop some very useful skills. Enjoy!

How it Works

You will see four icons at the top of each activity listed in this book—they will help you choose the right game for your child at the right time. Take a few moments to familiarize yourself with the key below. Have fun!

AGE You are the best judge of your own child's skills and abilities, but this is our recommended minimum age.

NUMBER OF PARTICIPANTS Many activities are great for your child on her own. Team games are better for parties.

GAME TIME How much of your time each activity requires—or how long it will occupy the kids so you can take a break!

EQUIPMENT NEEDED Ranges from three stars (a few household bits and pieces) to no stars (just your imagination).

1 Octopus Relay

You Need: ★ Two plastic soda bottles ★ Duct tape ★ Two buckets ★ A large container filled with water ★ Obstacles, such as chairs, toys, and a sprinkler

Create an "octopus" for each team by poking holes in the sides of the soda bottles and cutting the tops off, covering any sharp edges with duct tape. Set up an obstacle course and place the buckets—the same size for each team—at the end.

Each team fills its octopus in the container, runs through the course, and dumps into its bucket whatever water hasn't streamed out. The first team to fill its bucket wins.

2 Shark

One child gets to be the "shark," the others are "fish." Put hula hoops or beach towels on the ground to serve as dens for all the fish.

When the shark calls, *"Fishie, fishie, cross my ocean,"* the fish have to move to a different den. If, while out of a den, the shark tags them, they get to be sharks as well. The last remaining fish becomes the first shark next time. Adults can also remove dens, forcing kids to stand together on one.

★ The shark could instead be a dinosaur, dragon, or whatever you choose.

3 Mouse Tails

Tuck pieces of string or yarn about a foot long into the backs of the kids' shoes. After you say "Go!" the kids try to step on each other's tails. When all the tails are lost, replace and repeat.

. . . .

4 Tag

Someone is "it," and has to go "tag" everyone else. Try a variety of rules.

- ★ **Shadow Tag:** When "it" steps on your shadow, you're "it."
- ★ **Freeze Tag:** Freeze when tagged by "it."
- ★ **Blob Tag:** When you're tagged, you hold hands with "it" until everyone is connected in one big blob.

5 Graveyard Ghosts

One player is the "ghost." The rest lay down in a circle around her. They are now in the "graveyard." The ghost's job is to get the people in the graveyard to laugh or move without touching them. If someone does move or laugh, they become a ghost, too.

....

6 Simple Charades

Make a simple gesture and let your child guess what it is. For example, make a sandwich and eat it. When he's guessed correctly, reverse roles.

7 Red Light, Green Light

One player is the "traffic light." She stands 20 yards or more from the other players with her back turned toward them. The others are lined up behind her, shoulder to shoulder, aiming to get to the traffic light and tap her on the shoulder.

The traffic light starts the game by yelling *"Green light!"* The others run toward her until she yells *"Red light!"* and turns around as fast as she can. The instant the other players hear *"Red light!"* they must stop running. Anyone the traffic light sees still moving when she turns around must return to the starting line.

8 T-Ball

T-Ball is baseball for little kids. The rules are the same—you hit the ball and run the bases—but there is no need for a pitcher and catcher because a "tee" (a stand for the ball) is used instead.

This is a great game for birthday parties, family gatherings, and Sunday afternoons in the park because any number of people can play. A tee can be purchased fairly inexpensively at any toy store (or use a traffic cone!).

★ If there are only a few players, get a wiffle ball and bat so that the ball doesn't go very far.

9 Musical Chairs

Set out as many chairs as there are children, then put on lively music. Tell the kids to dance in a big circle until they hear the music stop, when they must—quickly, quickly!—find a chair and sit in it until the music resumes. With all the scrambling and squealing, you'd never guess there are always enough seats to go around.

10 Guessing Game

Use your fingertip and write a number or letter on your child's back. Ask him to guess what you've written. This is ticklish to some and they will laugh, but it's a fun way to learn numbers and letters.

11 Tug-of-war

You and your toddler each hold the end of a blanket and pull. Play this on a carpeted area and use it as part of an exercise routine. Both players sit in a straddle position. One person pulls gently on the blanket, stretching the other person forward until their hands are reaching toward (or ideally meeting) their feet.

. . . .

12 Basketball

Use a soft rubber ball or ball of yarn and a wastebasket as the basket. This is a great diversion if you need to distract a couple of kids quickly. Children can also play solo and try to beat their best score out of 20 shots.

13 Buttons and Beans

Mix different buttons or beans together and ask your kids to sort them by shapes or colors. Adult supervision is required for younger children.

14 Balloon Bean Bag

Cut three balloon-shaped holes out of large pieces of card. Paint around the holes with three different colors and glue on three pieces of yarn for balloon strings. When dry, prop up the cards and have the children play bean bag toss, trying to get the bean bags in the balloon-shaped holes.

15 Water Toys

Ask your child to pick small waterproofed objects from his toy box, light and heavy. Place one object after another into a container full of water. Watch how the toys behave in the water.

16 Scavenger Hunt

Challenge your toddler to go around the house and get something of a certain color—green, red, blue—and then increase the difficulty by asking for a number of things or by asking for things that start with a certain letter.

17 Duck, Duck, Goose

quack
quack

Players sit in a circle. One person is "it." She walks around the outside of the circle, gently tapping people on the head and saying "duck." But if she calls "goose," then that child has to get up and chase her. If the goose tags her before she gets back to the goose's spot, the goose sits back down. If "it" makes it to the free spot, then the goose becomes "it."

18 Backyard Campout

Set up a tent or a couple of sheets over a clothesline. Bring a picnic or, if your neighborhood allows, an adult can make a little campfire. Tell ghost stories and look at the stars. Sleep outside—even if it's just for a nap. This is a great "memory-building" time for family.

19 Wet Footprints

Cut several brown paper shopping bags at the seam so they can be spread out flat. Step into a shallow pan of water with bare feet and walk across the paper bag, leaving footprints. Watch as they evaporate and disappear. Repeat the activity making handprints. Try to cover the entire page before the prints evaporate.

20 Match Games

Buy two copies of the same magazine, cut out matching pictures, and glue them onto pieces of card. Scatter the cards face down on a table. Turn over two at a time, trying to find a matching pair. For a party, give each person a card to wear on their back and have the children find out which guests have matching pairs.

21 Twisting

Take a flat piece of fabric and stitch on a series of large (plate size) colored dots. Each player in turn is told to put, for example, their right foot on red or their left hand on green, until all the players are tangled together. The last person standing wins.

22 Follow the Leader

One person is the "leader" and the other children (or adults) follow the leader over obstacles, under furniture, or wherever! This is a great game for parties where kids are starting to get "on your nerves." Vary it by adding silly poses or movements.

....

23 Hide and Seek

Hide in the kitchen cabinets—or in the trees! Just make sure you have a boundary as to where little ones can go. If Mom is smart enough, she'll grab a magazine and hide somewhere really good—and get 10 minutes of alone time in the process!

24 Sock Match

Separate pairs of socks into two baskets. Place the baskets on different sides of the room. Have your active toddler pull a sock out of one basket and race to the other basket as fast as he can to find the matching sock.

....

25 Simon Says

Someone stands in front of the group and is "Simon." Simon then proceeds to tell the group to do things, like *"Touch your nose"* or *"Tap your head."* But players should only do it if Simon says the words *"Simon says"* first. If Simon doesn't say *"Simon says"* and you do it anyway, then you are out.

26 Roll those Big Dice

Wrap two medium-sized square boxes with white paper or wrapping paper turned inside out. Draw different colored shapes on the sides of the dice. Have your toddler roll each die and tell you what shape and color is on top.

27 Follow the Footprints

Draw some large footprints on craft paper. Cut them out and put them in a trail around the house. Tell your toddler that some strange creature has been walking around the place and you need to find him. Have your toddler follow the footprints to find a surprise... maybe a treat, or toy, or doll!

28 Giant Dominoes

You Need: ★ Cereal boxes ★ Black paper and white paint (optional)

Toddlers like to knock things down! This activity will let them do just that with some cereal box dominoes. Take a few of your empty cereal boxes and line them up on the floor. Push one at the end to show your toddler how they all fall down.

Your toddler will enjoy looking at the boxes and knocking them down. You can even put a rattle inside each box so that they make a noise when they fall over.

★ Try wrapping the boxes in black paper and painting them with domino dots.

29 Butterfly Numbers

You Need: ★ Four sheets of paper
★ Scissors ★ Coloring pens ★ Scotch tape

Draw and cut out four large, colorful butterflies, and number them 1 to 4. Now use a little tape to stick the four butterflies to a wall in order from left to right— 1, 2, 3, 4. Put them up just high enough that your toddler needs to reach up high to get them.

Ask your toddler to catch the butterflies. Each time he gets one, say the number on the card. When all four have been caught, celebrate with cheers and clapping.

30 Indoor Hopscotch

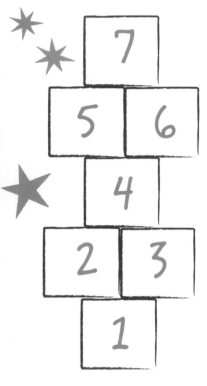

You Need: ★ Small toy
★ Masking tape

Take some masking tape and create a numbered hopscotch diagram on your floor. Then have your little toddler toss a small toy at the squares. Have her walk or jump over the squares to get to the toy and pick it up.

As she is jumping on each square, call out the number. Then have her bring the toy back to you and you take your turn!

★ This is a great way to get some exercise and learn your numbers, even if it's a rainy day!

31 Bottle Spin

Find an empty 12-oz plastic water or soda bottle. Now find some floor space where you can make a circle of board books. Put the bottle in the middle of the circle and spin it. When it stops, read the book the bottle is pointing to. Take turns spinning the bottle and reading. This makes reading fun and can be played with a group.

32 Toddler Twist

Put on some funky music and teach your toddler how to dance the "Twist" by twisting arms and body all around! Cut out some different color shapes (fairly large) and place them around the room on the floor. Have your toddler twist herself to a different shape and/or color.

33 Feeding Time

Buy some of those great animal paper plates, and tape them up on a wall. For food, use real snacks or crumble up some construction paper to make fake food.

Have your toddler "feed" each animal some food. Talk about the animal's name, color, and sounds. This is a great activity to get "non-eating" toddlers excited about eating. You can even cut out a small hole in the mouths on the plate to let your toddler put the food in.

★ This is also a great activity to introduce your toddler to the concept of sharing.

34 Walk, Count, March

It's time to get those legs moving and those fingers counting. Find some floor space and some great marching music and get marching!

35 Blue Egg, Red Egg

Put a row of colorful plastic or painted eggs into an egg container. Have your toddler put a matching colored egg in the cup next to each one. You can help, and when you do, keep saying the name of the color egg that you are looking for. When you find it, say that you found the "*blue egg*" and let your toddler place it in the cup next to the blue egg.

36 Egg Memory Game

Take five or six colorful plastic eggs and line them up on the floor. Open one of the eggs, saying the color ("*yellow egg*"), and put in a piece of black construction paper. Then close up the egg and mix the eggs up. Ask your toddler which one has the black paper in it. Then go through the colors and open up each one. When you find the paper, celebrate with a high five and do it again!

37 Egg Crawl

Find a box big enough for your toddler to sit down in. Pour a bag of plastic eggs into the box and let your toddler get in with them. As she tosses eggs out of the box, toss them back in and call out the color of the egg.

38 Balancing Act

Place a plastic cup upside down on the floor and balance a tinfoil pizza pan on top. Let your toddler put some magnetic letters on the pan to see how many he can put on before it falls down. Each time your child puts a letter on the pan, say the name of the letter.

39 Chalk It Up!

Find a safe area on the driveway or sidewalk where you can chalk simple shapes and objects. Use all sorts of colors and talk about them as you draw. When you are finished, ask your toddler to stand on the yellow flower, or the blue circle, or the pink butterfly. See if she can jump from one shape to another.

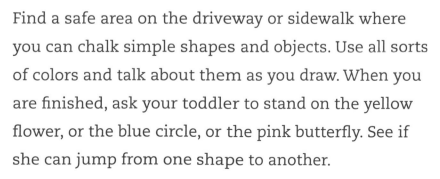

40 Jump Rope

You Need: ★ String or yarn ★ Masking tape

Find some string or yarn and cut a piece two feet long. Then tape the ends to the floor, rug, driveway, or sidewalk. Make sure the string is pulled tight so that it is flat on the ground and your child can't trip on it.

Ask your toddler to step over the piece of "rope." Then see if he can jump over the rope. You can even bring out some stuffed animals to help demonstrate how to jump over the rope. Take turns jumping over the rope.

★ For advanced jumpers, put down a few pieces of string about a foot apart so that your toddler can jump a few times in a row!

41 Hammer Colors

You Need: ★ A big pillow
★ Stickers ★ Toy hammer

This is a great activity for those toddlers that have an endless supply of energy. Find a big pillow and let your toddler put stickers all over it.

Locate your child's plastic toy hammer and let your child hit the stickers on the pillow to help get them to stick better. You can say, *"Hey Caitlin, try to hit that red flower sticker with the hammer,"* or *"Great job, Aiden, you really hit that blue circle sticker hard!"*

★ If you have alphabet stickers, this is a great way to introduce new letters or review old ones.

42 Counting Raisins

Draw small ovals all over a sheet of paper and put it down on your toddler's tray or table. Then put a snack of raisins on top of the small ovals. Let your toddler count the raisins as she gobbles them up!

43 Step Toddlerobics

Take those storage bins of different sizes you have full of stuff and turn them upside down. Leave about a foot between them and have your toddler step up, then down, and then up again, while holding your hand if necessary. He'll have a great time going up and down, and up and down.

44 Pumpkin Counting

Cut five pumpkin shapes out of orange felt. On each pumpkin draw a single Jack O'Lantern face with a large smile but no teeth. Number the pumpkins from one to five. Cut 15 tooth shapes out of white felt.

Place the pumpkins on a flannelboard. Have your children take turns identifying the numbers on the pumpkins and placing the appropriate number of teeth in each pumpkin's mouth.

45 Flashlight Fun

Before you start this activity, go into your child's room or some other room in the house and place some of his favorite toys and books around the room. To begin, review the idea of a lighted room and a dark room.

Let your little one turn the light switch off and turn the flashlight on. Ask him to try to find his teddy bear with the flashlight. As he swings the light around, you

can mention all the things you see until you get to the teddy bear, or whatever he was hunting for with the light. You can also review the different parts of a room—ceiling, floor, window, door, closet, bed, dresser—by flashing the light on each.

46 London Bridge

Two players become the towers of London Bridge. They clasp hands and raise them to form an arch. The rest of the players walk under the arch one by one, singing:

London Bridge is falling down, falling down, falling down,
London Bridge is falling down, My fair lady!

When they sing, "*My fair lady,*" the towers drop the arch and trap someone in their arms. This person then replaces the child who has been a tower for the longest amount of time, and the game continues.

★ There are no winners or losers; this game ends when the kids get tired of it.

47 Passing Parcel

You Need: ★ Small gifts ★ Gift wrap ★ Music

For this toddler party game, buy two or three little toys and wrap them up a good number of times. Seat the kids in a circle and have them pass around the present while the music is playing. When the music stops, have the child holding the present rip open the top layer. Then start the music again. Keep the present going around—whoever opens the final layer gets the present.

★ Try having two presents going around at the same time.

48 Bean Bag Toss

Purchase bean bags suitable for tossing, or create your own with dried beans, socks, and rubber bands. Draw a character or image on the side of a cardboard box. Cut a hole in the box, large enough for the bean bags to be thrown through easily. If you have drawn a character, the character's mouth can be the hole.

Place the box about 10 feet away and give each child several chances to toss the bean bags through the hole.

49 Parachute Play

Have the children stand and hold the edges of a large blanket. Place one stuffed animal or one lightweight ball in the middle of the blanket and have the children try to bounce it as high as they can, but without bouncing it off the blanket. Add more animals and balls to make the game more challenging.

50 All Change

A yard is better for this toddler party game as you need a bit of space. The children spread out and you call out two names of children who then have to run and change places. You or a selected child has to try and run to the spot that one of them has vacated. Don't try too hard!

51 Broken Bridges

You Need: ★ String ★ A wooden plank

For this all-action outdoor game, stretch two lengths of string across the lawn to represent the banks of a stream, with the plank joining the two banks.

Get the children to run round the garden and to "cross" the river via the plank. Turning your back on them, you then suddenly shout out *"Splash!"*—any child caught on the plank has to fall into the river and is out.

52 Cat and Mouse

Put on some music and the kids have to squeak and scuttle about like mice. The moment the music stops, the kids must be as still and as "quiet as a mouse." Anyone seen moving or making a noise is pounced on by the cat (you!) and is out of the game.

53 Copy Cat

Sit on a chair with the children sitting at your feet. Point to a part of your body and name it, followed by *"meow."* The children have to imitate you. For example, point to your chin and say, *"Chin, chin, chin, meow,"* and they all copy you. If you do the same, but don't say *"meow,"* any copycat who copies you is out.

54 Count the Pebbles

Sit all the children on the floor with their backs to you and stand behind them with a cookie tin. At irregular intervals, drop ten or more pebbles into the tin. The kids have to try and count them out loud and say the correct total. This can get very loud and confusing but the kids love it.

55 Musical Animals

Put on some music and get the kids to dance around. As you stop the music, hold up a picture of an animal such as a lion, pig, or dog. They then all have to jump around the room imitating that animal. Younger children love this game.

56 Down on the Farm

Prepare in advance a short story and include lots of animals and noisy farm vehicles. It doesn't have to be a very adventurous story as the point of the game is to make the noises of the animals and vehicles.

You could start with: "It was a beautiful sunny day down on the farm and the chickens (the kids: 'Cluck!') were wandering around the farmyard. Suddenly the big brown carthorse (the kids: 'Neigh!') came galloping over to Farmer Giles in his tractor (the kids: 'Vroom!')..."

57 Guess Who I Am

Think up in advance some characters or animals. With the kids all seated at your feet, you start to silently act out one of the characters or animals. Gradually you introduce some noises and the children have to guess who or what you are.

For example, if you were a cat you could run around on all fours, play with a ball of wool or an imaginary mouse, and then shout: *"Meow!"*

58 Bubbles, Bubbles

Toddlers just love bubbles. Give the adults present different bubble wands and solution. Count to three and begin creating bubbles. Your toddlers will have a wonderful time scrambling after them, counting how many they can catch.

59 Out of Doors

Make a conga line and jog gently around the yard singing a well-known nursery rhyme. You could end up at the sandpit or other activity area that you wish the children to get involved in.

60 Musical Shapes

Draw and color some big, basic shapes on large pieces of paper (e.g. yellow square, red triangle, green circle). Place these around the room where the children can see and reach them quite easily.

Start the children dancing to the music and when the music stops, shout out a color and shape such as *"yellow triangle."* The children have to rush to that color shape. The last one there is out of the game.

★ For a younger age group, stick to four or five color shapes.

61 Pair Them Up

In advance, collect pairs of a number of items such as socks, spoons, pencils, hair slides, or toy cars. Place one of each pair into paper bags or boxes equal to the number of children that are playing. The children don't all have to have the same items and sometimes you can repeat the game and allow five or six items per child. Hide the other halves of the pairs around the house. Issue each child with a bag or box and get them to go on a hunt for their matching halves. The first child to get a complete collection wins.

★ For two- to three-year-olds restrict this toddler party game to one room.

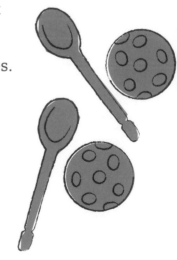

62 What's the Time, Mr. Wolf?

You or another child can play the part of the wolf. As the wolf walks away, the children all follow him then say loudly: *"What's the time, Mr. Wolf?"* The wolf turns slowly around and replies *"It's 3 o'clock"* or any time that he wishes.

When the wolf answers *"It's 12 o'clock... and dinner time!"*, the children have to run away with the wolf running after them. If he catches anyone, they become the next Mr. Wolf.

★ A good player of Mr. Wolf will create plenty of loud screams.

63 Old Soldier

One of the children pretends to be an old soldier, and goes around begging from each of the other players in turn. He says that he is poor, and old, and hungry, and asks what they will do for him or give him.

The players must answer the old soldier, but no one must say the words yes, no, black, or white. Anyone who does not reply at once, or who uses any of the forbidden words, must pay a forfeit.

64 Where's the Sock?

You Need: ★ Advertisements from magazines ★ Pins ★ Sock ★ Large sheet of paper

In advance, stick colored magazine advertisements for rooms of furniture on a large sheet of paper. Try and get it to look a little like your house—so, include a kitchen, bedroom, bathroom, and living room. Then hide a sock somewhere around the house.

Tell the children that the hostess has mislaid her sock and needs help to find it. The children then place pins on the picture where they think the sock might be. Then all the children run to their chosen place to see who was correct.

65 Fancy Foot

Set up a wading pool and let the kids paint the bottoms of their feet with washable paints. Let them step on paper to make their footprints, then hop in the pool, wash off, and start again. (Remember: always supervise around water.) Later, they can try to find their dry footprints by matching them up with their feet.

66 Jump the Puddles!

Get dressed in your rainboots and coats and go stomp in the puddles! You can have more fun by demonstrating how to drag your feet gently through the water. You could also play "follow the leader" or hold hands and jump with both feet into the puddles!

67 Spider Web

Attach each of a number of strings of varying lengths (one for each guest) to a small prize wrapped in tissue paper. Then hide the prizes around the house, and twine the strings around the furniture and into adjoining rooms, creating a spider's web.

Each child is given a string and proceeds to wind it around an empty spool or piece of pasteboard until a prize is reached. The strings must not be broken. An extra prize may be awarded to the child who first winds up a string neatly.

68 Bat Tag

Blindfold one child—she's the bat. The rest of the children are insects. Every time the bat says "*Beep, beep!*" the insects call back "*Buzz, buzz!*" while moving around. When the bat tags an insect, the insect has to go to the bat cave (say, the couch). The last insect standing becomes the next bat.

69 Family Trees

Hike through the woods or park with your child to find "baby" trees (short, with thin trunks) and "grandpa" trees (tall, with fat trunks). Find sizes in between for sisters, brothers, moms, dads, and grandmas. Compare their sizes by giving them hugs around their trunks.

70 So Big!

Check an encyclopedia or go online to find out with your child how tall his toy animals would grow in the wild. Draw a line outside with chalk. Take a stuffed animal (say, a giraffe), remind your child how tall it can grow (19 feet), and have him walk that many steps while you count together. Mark where he stops and leave the animal there.

Repeat with the others. Study your homegrown zoo together. Which is tallest? Which is smallest?

71 Nature's Treasure

When you're out, have your child fill each compartment of an egg carton with two of the same object, such as rocks, acorns, or leaves. Back home, look at, touch, smell, and talk about her finds. Tip them out and mix them up. Two- and three-year-olds will have fun trying to rematch the pairs. Give your four-year-old different ways to pair them up, such as hard and soft, living and non-living.

72 Can You Hear It?

Find a quiet spot outside where you can sit together. Close your eyes. Use your fingers to count all the sounds that you hear in one minute. Ask your toddler to tell you how many sounds he heard.

73 Carrot Scavenger Hunt

For an Easter game, cut out 20 carrots from orange construction paper and glue on green construction paper tops. "Plant" them all around the house—under cushions, in a drawer, or taped to the refrigerator door. Send your kids around the house to gather all the carrots. Let them redeem their carrots for snacks.

74 Easter Rabbit Hop

Choose three backyard landmarks, such as a picnic table, a tree, and a large rock. Have both teams line up at the same mark. Each player must hop on one foot to the second mark, skip from there to the third mark, and then jump back on two feet to tag the next teammate.

75 Easter Egg and Spoon

You Need: ★ Eggs ★ Spoons ★ Flags or markers

Each team stands in single file behind the starting line and opposite their respective flags, set in the ground about five yards away. At the whistle, the first player in each line, balancing an egg on a spoon, races around his team's flag, then back to transfer the egg onto a spoon held by the next teammate. The recipient races to the flag, and the first runner hands his spoon to the third person.

The race continues until one team finishes the course. Anyone who drops an egg must run to the starting line for another before resuming.

★ To make this game easier for tots, hard-boil the eggs, or use plastic ones.

76 Halloween Bat

Tape or tack a winding route of crepe paper around the ceiling of your party room. Find or purchase a mirror about six inches in diameter and affix it to a larger piece of cardboard on the floor. (This will block out some of the floor, allowing kids to concentrate on the upside-down route.)

To find their way through this bat cave, children must look down at the mirror and follow the route reflected from the ceiling. They will find themselves gingerly stepping around light fixtures, open doors, and any creepy decorations you have hung from the rafters.

eeek

77 Rolling Pumpkins

Line up two teams. The first person passes the pumpkin over his head to the next person in line. The next person passes the pumpkin under her legs to the next person, and so on. When you get to the end of the line, the last person runs back to the front and starts again, until the winning team is back in starting position.

78 Halloween Corners

Stick a Halloween-themed picture (witch, bat, ghost) in each corner . Play some music. When it stops, each child runs to a corner. Without looking, the music operator calls out one of the pictures ("*Ghost!*"). The children in that corner are out. The last person left is the winner.

79 Halloween Spiders

Make a set of four spider legs for each team: stuff two old pairs of tights and tie them together with string. Attach them to a belt.

Divide the children into two teams. The first player on each team straps a set of legs around her waist so that four legs will dangle on each side of her when she's in the classic crab position. On *"Go!"* the players scurry on all fours (eights including the spider legs!), with their bellies to the sky, to the line and back. Each team then helps its player take off the legs and strap them on the next runners. This continues until the final "spider" reaches the finish.

80 Pass the Pumpkins

You need a set of pumpkins or gourds, one less than there are children. Have the kids sit in a circle and pass these around when the music is playing. When the music stops, the child without a pumpkin is out. Remove one pumpkin. Continue until there's a winner.

81 Halloween Scarecrow

Find a variety of old clothes, pillowcases for heads, markers, and newspaper. Form the children into groups. The groups have 20 minutes to create their scarecrow. Give prizes to the scariest, then place outside.

82 Five Little Pumpkins

Ask your toddlers to count down on their fingers as they sing this song:

Five little pumpkins were sitting on a gate.
The first one said, "It's getting mighty late."
The second one said, "There are witches in the air."
The third one said, "I really don't care."
The fourth one said, "Let's run, run, run."
The fifth one said, "It's Halloween fun."
"WHOOO," went the wind, and out went the light,
And the five little pumpkins rolled out of sight.

★ For older toddlers, turn out the light on the second-to-last line.

86 Thanksgiving Photo

Use photographs of family members to prepare your child for Thanksgiving guests. Go through a photo album and talk about the people in the pictures. Can your child identify the same people in other photos?

87 Thanksgiving Nuts

Set out a bowl of unshelled mixed nuts and play these games with your child. Sort the nuts by kind or color. Count the number of pecans, the number of almonds, and so forth. Line up the nuts from smallest to largest. Supervise this game, as nuts can be a choking hazard, and remember to check for nut allergies.

88 Thanksgiving Turkey

Give your child some sheets of newspaper and a paper bag. Have your child crumple up the newspaper sheets and stuff them into the bag, pretending that they are stuffing the turkey. Can he count how many sheets it takes to stuff the turkey?

89 The Water Game

Place two pans on a table. Fill one halfway with water. Give your child a large turkey baster and show her how it works. The game is to transfer water from one pan to the other. Squeezing the bulb of the baster can help children develop the finger and hand muscles that are essential for writing skills.

90 Thanksgiving Food Fun

Thanksgiving is a great time for learning.

★ Discuss and explore with your toddlers the many food items made from corn.

★ Let your children help you measure ingredients for cooking projects.

★ Let them help you weigh a turkey (or other food item) at the store.

★ Help your toddlers discover what happens while food is cooking or freezing.

★ Teach your children to make butter.

★ Help your child divide items that are fruits from items that are vegetables.

91 Cookie Prints

Collect several Christmas cookie cutters. Place thin sponges in pie pans and pour on tempera paint in a selection of colors. Show your child how to press the cookie cutters onto the sponges, then onto paper to make a variety of holiday prints.

★ For gift wrap, print on large paper, such as butcher paper or brown wrapping paper.

★ Printing with red and green on newspaper is fun.

★ Create gift bags by printing on paper lunch sacks.

★ To make greeting cards, print on folded pieces of construction paper.

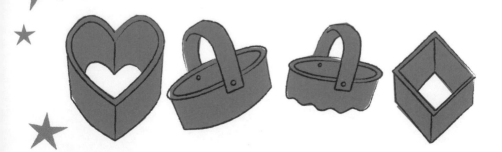

92 Christmas Card Throw

Divide a pile of Christmas cards of various sizes between the players. Have them stand in a circle about six feet from a laundry basket. They each throw their cards at the basket. The person who gets the most cards in the basket wins the game.

93 Christmas Wreath

Cut the center out of a small green paper plate. Invite your children to glue on Christmas-scented items such as dried orange peel, cinnamon sticks (broken into pieces), whole cloves, and peppermint candies. Add a red bow. Make a hanger by punching two holes in the top of your wreath and tying on red ribbon.

94 Christmas Countdown

Photocopy a December calendar page and let your toddlers decorate it with crayons or markers. Attach a holiday sticker on the 25th to mark Christmas Day. Each morning, give your children a sticker to attach on that day's date, counting down the days until Christmas.

★ 95 Wrap It Up!

Select a familiar object, such as one of your child's toys, and wrap it like a gift. Ask your child to feel the outside of the package and try to guess what's inside. Let her open the package to see if her guess was right. Then let her wrap an object for you to guess.

96 Ornamental Stories

Put several sturdy Christmas ornaments in a bag, and sit with your child. Reach into the bag, take out an ornament, and start telling a story about it. Then let your child take out an ornament and continue the story, making his ornament a part of it.

Take turns reaching into the bag and keeping the story going until all the ornaments have been used. Then bring the story to an end.

97 Christmas Spirit

Get into the holiday spirit with your child by trying these suggestions. Make cookies for a shut-in neighbor. Drop coins into a bellringer's kettle. Put a food item in a food donation bin. Take a new toy to a children's shelter.

98 Gift Game

Pass out keywords from a Christmas story, like "Twas the night before Christmas," then read the story. When you say a keyword in the story, the person holding the word yells "HO, HO, HO!" and gets to pick a gift.

99 The 12 Days of Christmas

Each of the 12 days of Christmas corresponds to a month of the year. The first day represents January, the second day is February, and so on. Sing the song. When the verse corresponding to your birthday month is sung, you stand up; when it's finished, you sit down. You stand up whenever the gift for that day is sung in the chorus.

So, if your birthday is in March, you stand for "On the third day of Christmas my true love sent to me, three French hens," and then when everyone sings "...four calling birds, [stand up] three French hens [sit down], two turtle doves..." Four or five verses into the song, you will have people popping up and down like crazy.

100 Reindeer Antlers

You Need: ★ Old pantyhose, one pair for each team ★ Balloons

Make two to four teams. Hand each team one pair of pantyhose. Hand out one balloon to each team player. If the teams are small, give two balloons per person (each team should have about eight balloons in total).

Jingle bells...

When you say *"Go"* the teams race to make "reindeer antlers" by blowing up the balloons and stuffing them into the pantyhose. Then one team member wears the antlers and sings "Jingle Bells." The first team to complete the task wins, but let everyone complete the task for a reindeer group picture.

101 I Packed Santa's Bag

Sit in a circle. The first person starts by saying "I packed Santa's bag and in it I put...", then they say what they put in it. The first item might be a teddy bear, but you can pack Santa's bag with anything. The person on their right follows, "I packed Santa's bag and in it I put a teddy bear and a fruitcake..." The third person says, "I packed Santa's bag and in it I put a teddy bear, a fruitcake, and a TV..."

This can go on for quite a while. You will find it amazing how many things you can remember. If you forget something, you are out.

102 Santa's Beard

Make two or more teams. On one side of the room put a big bowl of cotton balls for each team. Prepare the players by letting them put petroleum jelly all over their cheeks and chins. Be careful of eyes as usual.

The aim of the game is to run to the other side of the room, stick your face in the bowl of cotton balls, and then run back wearing your Santa beard so the next person can go. The winning team is the one who collects the most cotton balls in the time allowed.

Ho ho ho

103 Snowflake Match

Gather together scissors, blue and white construction paper, and glue. Cut ten matching snowflake shapes out of white paper, then cut ten matching snowflakes of a different shape. Next, cut squares from the blue paper, making them slightly larger than the size of your snowflakes. Glue the snowflakes onto the blue squares.

To Play:

1. Spread the game pieces out onto a flat surface with the snowflakes facing down.
2. To start the game, have your preschooler pick one of the game cards and carefully look at the shape of it.
3. Ask your preschooler to turn over two snowflakes and see if they match. If they do, she keeps them. Then it's your turn, but you have to collect snowflakes of the other shape.
4. Continue playing until you each have a matching set of snowflakes.

104 Chubby Little Snowman

Look at some pictures of snowmen in books or magazines before doing the actions to this poem:

A chubby little snowman
Had a carrot nose. (POINT TO YOUR NOSE)
Along came a bunny (HOP AROUND THE ROOM)
And what do you suppose?
That hungry little bunny
Was looking for some lunch.
Took that snowman's nose
(PRETEND TO GRAB YOUR CHILD'S NOSE)
Nibble, nibble, crunch!

105 Melting Snow

Give each child a plastic cup. Ask them to fill the cups with snow (or ice), bring them inside, and place them around the room. Ask them to check their containers periodically to see what is happening to the contents.

106 Indoor Snowmen

Make snowmen out of white paper plates. Take one plate for the body of each snowman and cut a second plate into a smaller circle for the head. Tape them together. Glue real buttons on the body. Use construction paper to make the snowman's hat. Then use a marker to draw the face. Be creative and use whatever you can find in your craft bin. Then have a snowman party!

107 Christmas Decorations

Preheat the oven to 350°F. Wrap the sides and bottoms of several Christmas cookie cutters with aluminum foil. Place the cookie cutters on a baking sheet, foil side down, and spray the insides of each one with cooking spray.

Put about five or six colored candies in each cookie cutter. Place the cookie sheet in the oven for ten minutes. Poke a hole through the top of each ornament with a toothpick while the candy is still slightly warm.

When completely cooled, carefully remove the ornaments from the cookie cutters. Thread a piece of ribbon through the hole at the top of each one and hang them on your Christmas tree.

Creating
& Imagining

108 Spray It!

Fill a spray bottle with a little water and send your toddler off to clean all the "dirt" off the wall. This is a great way to distract your toddler while you really clean the bathroom.

109 Cat Bat

Ask the children to pretend to be cats. Hang a piece of string from the ceiling, just out of the children's reach, and tell them to bat at the string with their "paws."

110 Ant Farm

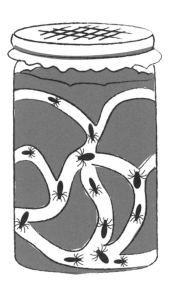

You Need: ★ A glass jar
★ Black paper ★ Nylon stocking
★ Rubber band ★ Soil ★ Ants!

Fill the glass jar with loose soil and ants. Use the rubber band to secure the stocking on the top of the jar and cut off the excess, leaving a good amount around the edge so you can easily take it off and put it on the jar again.

Tape black paper around the outside of the jar so the ants will build tunnels on the sides of the jar. Don't forget to feed and water your new pets. After a couple of hours, take off the paper and see what is happening. Don't forget to put the paper back on the jar.

111 Ant Picnic

Divide a paper plate into sections with a black marker. Place various food items on the plate (e.g. crackers, sugar, lettuce). Set the plate outside on a nice warm day, in a quiet shaded area where you have seen ants.

Check back after one hour to see what has happened. Check again after two hours. Which foods have the ants taken and which have they left?

★ Ask your children what foods the ants like the best.

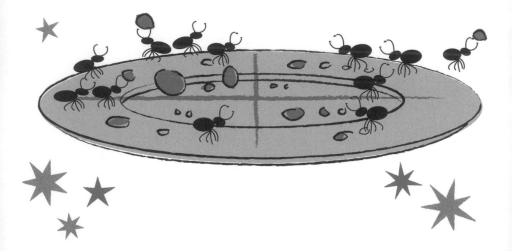

2+ 1+ 30 **

112 Grocery Store

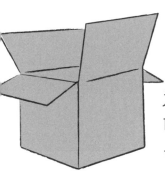

No need to buy anything—just collect the boxes you already have: macaroni boxes, spaghetti boxes, jello boxes, dry soup boxes, cookies boxes, crackers boxes. Use play money to shop at the grocery store.

2+ 1+ 60 *

113 Furry Bird

Cut the shape of a bird out of an old cardboard box. Go on a nature hunt and gather up some feathers. Let the children glue feathers to the bird. Tell them the names of the birds the feathers came from, and ask them to make up a name for their bird.

114 Bird Mask

Have the children paint a paper plate with a bird face. When dry, glue on feathers and a cardboard beak. Cut out holes for the eyes and glue a popsicle stick to the back for a handle. Let's play at birds...

115 Birdseed Collage

Gather together paper, glue, and birdseed. Work with your child to use the birdseed to create a collage. Make a round sun in the sky, and use little "V" shapes of glue and birdseed to create birds in the sky.

116 Hand Turkey

Paint the palm and thumb of your child's hand brown. Then paint each of their fingers a different bright color. Have her press her hand onto a piece of white paper. The thumb represents the turkey's neck and the palm the body. Draw on feet, eyes, and beak.

....

117 Trace the Turkey

Help your child trace their hand onto a piece of paper and then draw in the features of a turkey. Make up a story about the turkey as you color it in.

118 Feather Headbands

Measure your child's head and cut out a piece of construction paper long enough to create a headband. Glue the paper together so the headband fits snugly on your child's head but is loose enough to take off easily. Glue feathers to the headband. Let's play the Wild West.

119 Pinecone Bird Feeder

Cut a long piece of yarn or ribbon. Tie the ribbon in a knot around a pinecone, near the top. Spread peanut butter on the pinecone, then sprinkle birdseed over it. Hang your bird feeder on a tree.

120 Vinegar and Eggs

Place a hard-boiled egg in a cup of vinegar and see what happens. (It bubbles!) After one day, take out the egg, wipe it off with a paper towel and feel the egg. Ask your toddlers questions about what you see and feel.

....

121 Nesting Hen

Place some plastic eggs under a pillow. Have your toddler sit on the pillow like a nesting hen and guess how many eggs are under the pillow. Then count the eggs along with your child.

122 Baby Bird

Stand the children in a circle, with one child (the "baby bird") in the middle. Secretly give one of the children in the circle a gift to hold behind his back.

The baby bird points at someone in the circle and says, "*Are you my mother?*" If the child has the gift, they answer "*Yes,*" and hand it over. If the child does not, the children pass the gift around behind their backs, or pretend to. Then baby bird guesses again.

He has three guesses to win the prize, before it is someone else's turn to be baby bird.

Are you my mother?

123 Balloon Car

Cut off the lip of a balloon. Cut a drinking straw in half. Stick the straw into the balloon and tape it in place, making a tight seal. Tape the straw to the top of a toy car with the straw pointing back. Blow up the balloon through the straw and seal the balloon by pinching the straw. Set the car down on a smooth surface and let go.

124 Train Movement

Divide the children into three groups. Have each group form a "train" with their hands on the shoulders of the person in front of them. Instruct the children to move around the room (or yard) and remain connected. Every minute or two, switch engines.

125 Color Train

Cut out "tickets" from different-colored sheets of construction paper. Give each child three or four tickets. Tell them that you are the conductor of the Color Train and they can only ride the train if they have a ticket that matches the color you call. Set up some chairs in a line, with your chair at the front.

Announce *"All aboard the Red Train,"* or the color of your choice. Have the children give you their ticket and then clamber into a chair. After a minute or two, announce a new color.

★ Vary the game by using numbers, letters, or shapes instead of colors.

126 Clickety Clack

Have the children spread out around the room. Pick one child to be the engine of the train. Give each child a ticket with a number on it. The ticket should be large enough so the number can be clearly seen. Have the child who is the engine pick up the passengers in order.

127 Whistle Game

Have all the children line up and make a train. Instruct them that one short whistle means "Stop" and two short whistles means "Go slowly." If they do well with the two signals, add more: three whistles means "Back up," one long whistle means "Stop and turn," and so on.

128 Train Sort

Set up boxes to make them look like train cars. Supply the children with different things (cargo) to sort into the boxes. Ask them to sort by color, shape, or texture. Or let them sort and tell you how they chose to sort the items.

129 Number Train

Cut out a train engine and five boxcar shapes from construction paper. Number the cars from one to five, then ask the children to line up the cars in order. Add magnets to the boxcar shapes and stick them to the door of your refrigerator.

1 2 3 5 4

130 How Far Will it Go?

Place a toy train at the top of a ramp and ask the children how far it will go. Record their answers with masking tape labels with each child's name on them. Try this on carpet first and then switch to a smooth surface. Give prizes for the closest guesses.

131 Boxcar Train

Connect three or four boxes together to form a train for the children to play in. For a longer activity, help the children to decorate the boxes like a train engine and its cars, and paint numbers on the cars.

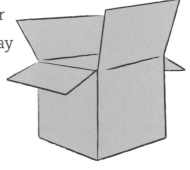

132 Teddy Bear Train

Find a box that a teddy bear will fit into. Help your child decorate the box as desired. Poke a hole in the box big enough to thread a piece of yarn through. Tie on a piece of yarn, just long enough for the child to hold, while the box rests on the floor. Let the child pull the train around with their teddy bear aboard.

133 Balloon Fun

Inflate a balloon. Stretch the neck of the balloon so the air escapes slowly causing the balloon to "sing" or vibrate. Inflate the balloon again. Ask your child, "What will happen if I let go?" Let go…

134 Balloon Chair

You Need: ★ 20–30 small balloons
★ Large garbage bag

★ Fully inflate a balloon. Ask your child what will happen if she sits on it. Let your child try it. If it doesn't pop, have her jump on the balloon to pop it.

★ Inflate enough of the balloons to fill the garbage bag. Help your child stuff the balloons into the bag, supervising her at all times. Seal the bag and have your child sit or even jump on their new balloon chair to see what happens.

135 Balloon Tap ★ ★

Count how many times you and your child can tap a balloon before it touches the ground. Use a watch or stopwatch to time yourselves and see how long you can keep the balloon in the air.

136 Balloon Sort

Have your child sort inflated balloons by their color, shape, or size. You can also count the number of balloons in each group.

137 Static Balloons

Help your child to learn about static electricity by rubbing a balloon on a child's head, then sticking it onto the wall. Hold contests to see how long a balloon will stick. Rub the balloon on a child's head again, and see who can lift up the highest hair!

....

138 Square Balloons

Half fill a balloon with water. Place the balloon in a square container, then place in the freezer. When it's frozen, take the balloon out of the freezer. Show your toddler what you have done. Ask them what will happen when the ice melts. Find out!

139 Balloon Color Chart

Make a large wallchart that has a column for each color of balloon that you are using.

Give each child two or three balloons. Have one child at a time tape their balloons to the chart according to color. Then after all the balloons are taped to the chart, count up each column.

★ How many red balloons are there? How many blue balloons? And so on.

140 Balloon Kites

This is a great birthday party activity. You will need large, round helium balloons, kite string, and paper streamers or ribbons. Tie one end of a long length of kite string to a round helium balloon and the other to your child's wrist. He will find it fun and easy to fly his balloon. Attach ribbons for an authentic kite look.

141 Search for Fossils

Place dried pasta noodles in a sandtable or sandpit. Hide the pasta in the sand and ask the children to look for the "dinosaur fossils." Piece together the fossils into a dinosaur shape and tell dinosaur stories.

142 Where's Your...?

Ask the children, "*Where's your* _____?"
Fill in the blank according to their age. How many of the following do they know?

Easy: Head, eyes, nose, foot.

Medium: Fingers, ankles, knees, neck, forehead.

Hard: Knuckles, wrist, thigh, forearm, palm, spine.

143 What's in the Sock?

Find a very colorful sock. Place something in the sock, like a block, or a toy. Let your toddler feel the object and try to guess what it is. Try with different objects.

144 What Scent is This?

Gather four or more different objects with different scents, like vanilla, mint, lemon, and popcorn. Wearing a blindfold, with the object close to his nose, can your toddler identify the objects using his sense of smell?

145 What Taste is This?

Gather four or more different foods with different tastes. Wearing a blindfold, can your toddler identify what the food is using her sense of taste? (Take care when choosing items for children to taste because some children may have allergies.)

146 Telescope Fun

You Need: ★ Empty toilet paper rolls ★ Cellophane wraps in a variety of colors ★ Rubber band or masking tape

To make a telescope, wrap a square of the cellophane around the end of the toilet paper roll and secure with the rubber band or tape.

Give each child a different-colored telescope. Have them all look through the tube to see what everything looks like. Ask them to shout out what they see. Then get them to trade telescopes with a friend.

★ This is a good game for a pirate-themed party, and the telescopes are a great party favor!

147 Wet or Dry

Wearing a blindfold, have your children touch a variety of different fabrics that are wet (with water) and dry. Can they guess whether they are wet or dry? This is harder than it sounds with some materials.

148 Milky Rainbows

Provide your toddlers with a shallow container of milk. Place a couple drops of different food coloring in the milk. Have them dip a toothpick into some soap solution and then dip it into the milk. Amazing! Try it again!

149 Sound Jars

Gather together empty film bottles or baby food jars. Place matching objects, like two coins, rice grains, dice, or pasta pieces, in pairs of containers. Seal the containers with colored contact paper.

Pick up one of the containers and shake it. Pick up another bottle and shake it. Then shake the first again. If they sound different, shake your head and say *"No!"* Shake bottles and compare them until they match, when you nod your head and say *"Yes!"* Place the two bottles side by side. Invite the children to help until all of the matches are found.

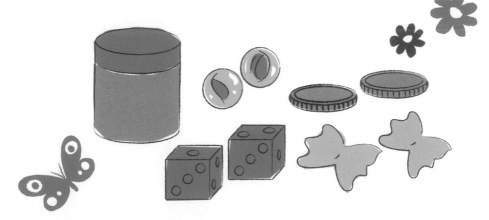

150 Count the Seeds

Before you cut an apple, have your child try to guess how many seeds will be inside. Cut open the apple and count them. Write down your child's guess, and the real answer. Repeat the next day. Compare results. Were there more, less, or the same?

151 Different Apples

Next time you go to the grocery store with your child, point out all the different kinds of apples. Tell your child their names. Buy a few different kinds, and when you get home, let your child try them. Ask your child how each one tastes.

152 Apple Sequencing

Gather three to five different-sized apples. Set them on a table and ask your child to arrange the apples according to size. For younger children, you can just start with two apples and ask which is the smallest.

153 Ladder Fun

Lie a ladder flat on the floor. Hold the ladder and have one child at a time walk between the rungs without touching the ladder. Then have them try walking on the rungs. This is great for a firefighter-themed party.

154 Mudpie Bakery

You will need dirt or sand and some water. Find a comfortable place to sit by a sandbox or a mud puddle and mix up a batch with the hand. Scoop and mold it into smooth "pies" and set them out to dry in the sun. Add twigs for birthday candles and celebrate a pretend birthday. Sprinkle with dry sand or dirt for sugar cookies. Decorate the pies with pebbles and leaves.

155 Post Office

Make a mail box out of a cardboard box. Use note paper and envelopes for mail. Rubber stamps and ink pads are great for postage stamps. Each child can have their own shoebox—decorated to their liking—for incoming mail.

156 Songs from a Hat

Write down the names of songs you sing on a regular basis. Place them into a hat. Have a child pull out the name of a song and then sing it.

157 Song Cube

Make a cube from a cardboard box. Place Velcro on each side. Write the names of songs you sing on pieces of

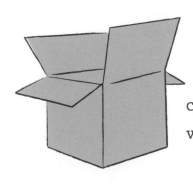

paper, laminate them, and add Velcro. Place one song on each of the cube's six sides. Have the children roll the cube and sing whatever song comes up on top.

158 Body Part Stickers

Give each child a sticker. Have them place the sticker on various parts of their bodies. Sing this song as they do it:

There is a sticker on my nose, on my nose, on my nose

There is a sticker on my nose, on my nose, on my nose

There is a sticker on my nose... and that's the way it goes!

There is a sticker on my chin, on my chin, on my chin

There is a sticker on my chin, on my chin, on my chin

There is a sticker on my chin... open my mouth, don't let it in!

★ Make up more rhyming lines together for other body parts.

159 Jiggle Giggle

Play some bouncy music. Have the children stand facing you, and ask them to jiggle the body part you call out. Start with easy ones like arm or head, then move on to harder body parts (e.g. calf or thigh).

160 Tightrope Walking

Place a strip of masking tape or a piece of yarn on the floor for the children to walk along. Ask them to stretch out their arms and imagine that they are a tightrope walker, balancing high up in the circus tent.

161 Sticky Tape

Cut strips of sticky tape and partially attach them to the edge of a table. Use the tape to identify body parts. Ask the children to place a piece of tape on the body part you name. (e.g. *"Place tape on your nose...."*)

162 See and Say

With the children sitting in a circle, give commands such as *"Touch your fingers to your toes"* or *"Put your hand on your thigh."* When the children can do this well, give two instructions at once: *"Put one hand on your head and the other hand on your tummy."*

163 Magic Bag

Fill a bag with fun things like balls, building blocks, toys, and fruit. Ask the toddlers to reach into the magic bag and pull out an item, identify it and demonstrate what they can do with it.

164 Shaving Cream

Take a wet paper towel and wet the table first. Put smocks on the toddlers and place a small dollop of shaving cream on the table. Encourage the children to cover the entire surface of the table with the shaving cream—but not lick their fingers!

165 Sandpaper Letters

Stencil the letters of the alphabet onto sandpaper. Cut the letters out and stick them onto cards. Place the cards in a bag. Ask the children to reach into the bag and feel for a card. Once they have found one, encourage them to feel the letter and guess what it is before pulling it out. Then they can pull the card out and check.

★ At first, choose only three or four letters and ask the children to read and feel them before putting them in the bag and playing the game.

166 Wet and Dry

Cover a table with newspaper. For each child, place a tray of sand and a cup of water on the table. Ask the children to pour the cup of water slowly into their trays. Talk about the changes in texture and how it feels (wet, mushy, cold).

167 Make a Box

A fabulous imagination builder! Grab a couple of shoeboxes and make up some different activities for each box. Here are some examples: Doll box—a small doll with clothes, a bottle, bibs, and a baby spoon. Art box—construction paper, scissors (kidsafe of course!), gluestick, dot painters, rubber stamps, washable inkpad.

168 Driving the Bus

You Need: ★ A large cardboard box
★ Scissors ★ Different-colored paints

Find a large cardboard box and cut off the top flaps. Help the children to paint the box the colors of a school bus, or other colors to make a regular bus. When the paint is dry, one child can hop in and start to drive.

★ If there are lots of children, ask them to form a circle around the bus. Each child gets a turn to drive and tell the others where they are going.

All aboard!

169 Shape Train

Give each child a large piece of white paper. Then give them rectangles and circles cut out of colored paper (this could be a separate activity). Help the children to lay out the shapes in a train pattern on the white paper. Glue the shapes in place.

170 House Collage

Cut out an assortment of magazine pictures of household objects. Hold them up and ask the children to identify them. Ask the children to select the objects they want and paste them onto a paper house shape.

171 Sailboats

To the tune of "Frère Jacques," teach the children to sing the following words:

> Boats are sailing, boats are sailing,
>   In the sea, in the sea.
> Floating all around us, floating all around us,
>   Look and see, look and see.

As the children sing the main part of the song, tell them to move around the room pretending to be sailing boats on the water. At the end of the song, show the children how to look out to the sea to spot other boats.

172 Ice Cube Racers ★

Use food coloring to make different-colored ice cubes using ice-cube trays. Set up an ice-cube racetrack by placing one end of a smooth board against the seat of a chair. Each child chooses an ice cube, puts it at the top of the racetrack and watches it race to the bottom.

173 Feely Bug

Cut a large bug shape out of cardboard. Cut out pieces of various materials (sandpaper, corduroy, wool, velvet, foam, cotton balls, felt) and ask the children to glue them on to the bug.

174 Guess the Insect

Show the children pictures of insects such as bees, grasshoppers, and ants. Ask the children to imitate you as you demonstrate the movement of each insect. For example, buzz around the room with arms extended like a bee, jump around on two feet like a grasshopper, and crawl around on all fours like an ant.

Take one child to the side and show him a picture of one of the insects. Then ask the child to move like the insect while the other children guess what it is.

175 Bug Identification

Cut out pictures of various bugs (spiders, bees, flies, beetles, ants) from magazines. Give the pictures to the children. Ask them to go outside and see if they can find bugs that match the pictures.

176 Follow the Light

Turn out the light and use a flashlight on the floor and walls. See if the toddlers can catch the ball of light.

177 Discovering Smells

Take all the condiments out of the refrigerator. Open them one at a time and let the children smell them. Discuss what things are called, their color, their smell, their taste, who likes what, etc. You can also do this with all your herbs and spices.

178 Stack 'em Up

Use stacking or measuring cups for this activity. Starting with the largest cup turned upside down on the bottom, show your toddler how to stack the cups from largest to smallest. Then turn the cups upright and stack them back together in a nest.

179 Fall Leaf Hanging

Collect a variety of colorful fall leaves and lay them out on a table. Give each child a 6–10 inch square of clear, self-stick paper with the backing removed. Let the children arrange the leaves on the sticky sides of their square of paper.

When each child is finished, place a second square of clear, self-stick paper over the first square and seal the edges well. Punch two holes at the top of each square and add a loop of yarn. Arrange the decorative leaf hangings in a window.

180 Leaf Spray

Fill several spray bottles with paint in a variety of fall colors. Tape leaves to sheets of paper and spray away. When the children are finished spraying, take the leaves off and see the results.

181 Windy Ping-Pong

Stick a strip of masking tape halfway across a small tabletop. This is your "net." Two children blow a ping-pong ball back and forth across the net, or squeeze two empty detergent bottles to create wind for a game of windy ping-pong.

182 Fall Walk

Give each child a paper bag with their name printed on it. Go for a walk and collect leaves, acorns, moss, and other items that you find. When you get back, ask the children to take turns showing what they have collected and display the items on a table.

183 Let Nature do the Talking

One evening, sit with your child in your backyard and watch the stars and the moon. Listen to the crickets. Watch the lightning bugs. You'll learn a lot about nature and a lot about each other, too!

184 Flower Wagon

Little kids like little things, and children will love having their own small garden in a wagon. You can use flowers or vegetables to create this garden.

Buy a child's wagon and drill a few holes in the bottom for drainage. Fill the wagon three-quarters of the way with soil. Let your child pick the flowers and help to plant them. Pansies, lavender, zinnias, marigolds, and primroses are all good choices.

★ Show your child how to water and weed the garden. It can even be taken for a walk to show friends.

185 Garden of Garbage

You Need: ★ An old garbage bin ★ Garden and kitchen waste

This garden will teach your child about composting.

Put the old garbage bin at the far side of the yard. Ask your child to help put some torn-up newspaper, old leaves and plants, grass clippings, and dirt on the bottom. Then start adding fruit and vegetable peelings, eggshells, and other uncooked vegetable waste.

Every few days stir it up. Let your child look in and smell nature at work! In a few weeks, worms and insects will turn it into fresh dirt for a new gardening project.

186 Family Puzzles

Take photos of your children. Glue each photo to a piece of cardboard and cover with clear, self-stick paper. Cut each photo into two or three simple puzzle shapes and place them in an envelope. Let the children select a photo puzzle and put it together.

· ·

187 Family Picture Tree

Cut from magazines different pictures of daddies, mommies, brothers, and sisters. Give each child a tree shape and paper leaves. Have them paste individual pictures of daddies, mommies, brothers, and sisters onto the paper tree and leaves.

188 Worm Farm

You Need: ★ A large cardboard box ★ Worms
★ Soil, kitchen scraps, and wet newspaper

By having her own worm farm, your child will learn how earthworms break down soil. To create your farm, find a large cardboard box and punch holes in the lid. Put soil, kitchen scraps, and wet newspaper on the bottom. Place the box in a cool, shady area of the yard.

Add your worms (dig them up or purchase them at your local nursery) and cover with a layer of wet newspaper and soil. Sprinkle with water and cover with the lid. Every few days, lift the lid and let your child find the worms in the soil.

189 Flower in a Shoe

Kids love sunflowers, and your child will love having his own sunflower shoe. Find a pair of old, tall boots (look in your basement or at a garage sale) and fill them with soil. Your child can decorate the boots before you fill them with dirt if he would like.

Place two sunflower seeds in each boot. Place the boots in a sunny location, water daily, and watch the flowers grow. Will they get taller than your child?

190 Which One's Different?

Lay out three objects the same color and one object a different color. Tell the children that one object is not the same color as the others. Ask the children to point to the object that is not the same color. Repeat with another series of objects.

191 Have You Grown?

Ask your child to lie on the floor as you stretch some thread from head to toe. Cut and place the thread in an envelope with your child's name on it. Do it again every few months and compare. You could record the measurements in a growth journal.

192 Feather Feet

Remove the feathers from several feather dusters. Put them in a big cardboard box. Remove your toddler's shoes and socks. Let them walk barefoot in the feathers. Then let them walk on a hard floor. Talk about the difference between how the soft feathers feel and how the hard floor feels.

193 Elevator Game

Ask the toddlers to pretend to go up and down in an elevator. As they go up, show them how to raise their arms and bodies up until they are on their tiptoes. Then show them how to go down in the elevator, lowering their bodies to the floor.

194 Newspaper Pillow

Lay out sheets of newspaper and pillowcases. Show the children how to crumple up the newspaper and stuff it into the pillowcases. Encourage them to crumple the newspaper quickly, slowly, noisily, and quietly. Continue putting it into the pillowcases until they are full.

195 Guess What I Am?

One child states they are either a person, place, or thing. The others then ask questions ("*Are you blue?*" "*Can you speak?*" "*Do you bark?*" "*Can you be eaten?*") The first child to guess correctly wins, and it is her turn to choose something or someone to "be."

196 Find a Shape

When learning shapes, begin with the circle. Cut circles out of cardboard. Give each child a circle. Take a walk around your house. When you find a circle, tape the cardboard circle on it. How many circles can you find? Repeat with different shapes.

197 Sponge a Shape

Cover a table with newspaper and put smocks on the children. Cut sponges into different shapes. Put different-colored paint into pie pans. Give each child a sheet of paper and print away!

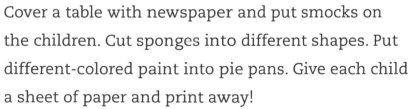

198 Feel a Shape

Cut different shapes out of cardboard.
Find a variety of materials of various
textures (sandpaper, corduroy, foam, velvet, silk,
cotton wool, felt). Cut shapes out of them to match
the cardboard shapes.

Lay the cardboard and material shapes
out on a table. Ask the children to find
a material shape that matches a
cardboard shape and glue them
together to create "feely" shapes.

★ If you use large pieces of
   cardboard, stick them low on
   the walls for the children to
   explore on their own.

199 Obstacle Course

Set up an obstacle course using a table, jump rope, chair, etc. Give short directions, such as "Crawl under the table," "Walk around the rope," "Sit on the chair," and "Crawl over the table."

200 Animal Weigh

Set out an infant scale or kitchen or bathroom scale. Let the children use it to weigh dolls and stuffed animals.

201 Color Book

Take six pieces of white paper. At the top of each piece, write the name of a color. On each page, ask your child to draw a picture using a crayon in the page's color. Glue in a piece of material or thread in the same color. Cut out and stick on objects in the color. Then start on the next page with a different color.

When there are several pages, make them into a book. Punch out holes and fasten the book together by tying ribbon or thread through the holes.

202 Ribbon Color Game

Put a variety of colored ribbons in a basket. Let each child select a ribbon. Help the children look around the room for objects that are the same color as their ribbon.

203 Cleaning Up

For this game you will need a laundry basket and some soft toys. Place the toys on the floor near the laundry basket and show your toddler how to put them into the basket. When you have finished, put the toys out on the floor again and start over.

204 Cats Sleep Anywhere

Read the poem about cats:

> Cats sleep anywhere, any table, any chair,
> Top of piano, window-ledge,
> In the middle, on the edge,
> Open drawer, empty shoe,
> Anybody's lap will do.
> Fitted in a cardboard box,
> In the cupboard with your frocks,
> Anywhere! They don't care!
> Cats sleep anywhere.

Pretend to be a cat and "meow" around the room. Ask a child to be the cat and give directions where to sleep, such as "Kitty cat, can you sleep under the table?"

205 Someone Else's Shoes

Take dressing up to a whole new level by allowing children to try on each other's shoes—and your own.

Put all the children's shoes in the middle of the room. Add other shoes (doll's shoes, ballet shoes, rubber boots, horseshoes, etc.) for fun. Add your own shoes, too. The children will have fun comparing and contrasting their own shoes to their friends' shoes.

★ Make a chart that shows which shoe is the biggest and which shoe is the smallest.

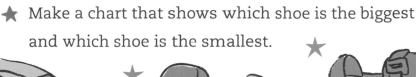

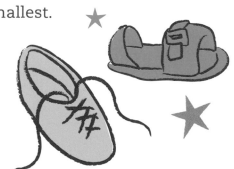

2+ 3+ 30 **

206 Dress Up!

Playing dressing up is something toddlers love to do.
As you discuss various clothes, you are developing
their language and adding to their vocabulary.

Gather together all kinds of clothing: hats, scarves,
shoes, gloves, or whatever you think that your toddler
would enjoy. Put on one of the hats and say, *"This hat
keeps my head warm."* Put on a glove and say, *"This glove
keeps my hands warm."*

Encourage your child to pick an article of clothing.
Help to name and describe it if necessary.

207 Blocks

Make disposable blocks out of small milk cartons (make sure they are completely clean and dry). Tape the ends closed and cover the cartons with paper. Let your toddler decorate the blocks with crayons or stickers.

Now play a stacking game with your toddler, trying to stack one block on another. Sometimes it might be more fun to knock down the stacks. The great thing about these blocks is that you can throw them away when they get worn out.

★ Decorating the blocks and stacking them help develop fine motor skills.

208 Fly Little Bird

Stand and face your toddler. Take his hands in yours. While holding hands, walk around in a circle and sing or say the following:

> Fly, little bird, through the window. (PRETEND TO FLY)
> Fly, little bird, through the door. (PRETEND TO FLY)
> Fly, little bird, through the window.
> Fly and touch the chair.

On the words "fly and touch the chair," pretend to fly and touch a chair. Ask your toddler to do the same thing. Sing the song again but fly and touch something different.

209 Ballapalooza

For this game you should collect at least four balls of different sizes. It's best to play outside, but if you are careful it can be played inside. Line up the balls in order of size and talk about how one ball is bigger or smaller than another. You can also comment on the color of each ball. Then roll the balls, carefully pass the balls, or gently kick the balls to each toddler.

★ There are always ways to bring learning into regular play. Just keep it fun!

210 What Do You See?

For this game you will need a mirror on the wall.

Lift your toddler up to the mirror and look into it together. Say something like: *"Look in the mirror, what do you see?"* Then point out all the different things you can see. Start by pointing to parts of the body, such as eyes, ears, hair, or nose. Then point to items of clothing and other things you can see in the mirror.

When your toddler is starting to say some words, point to parts of their body and ask what they are called.

211 Broom Tag

All you need is a broom and four or more children.

The child who is "it" is called the "Broom Chaser." She tries to tag other children with the end of the broom. If they are tagged, they join "it" in a team. They have to grab someone and yell *"Broom Chaser!"* Then "it" tags the person that's being held. Everyone who's tagged joins the team with "it."

When everyone is tagged except one person, the game is over and the person that is left becomes "it."

212 Beanbag Catch

For this game you will need different colored beanbags, for example red, pink, blue, yellow, and purple. Sit on the floor beside your toddler and play catch. As you gently pass a beanbag, say what color it is.

213 Block Towers

For this game you will need a set of blocks. They can be alphabet wooden blocks, plastic blocks, or even soft blocks. Show your toddler how to stack a tower two, three, and four blocks high. Keep building for as long as you would like!

214 Off and On

Play this game when it's dark. Ask the children to sit on the floor. Stand by a light switch and turn it off and on. As the lights go off, tell everyone to say "Off." As the lights go on, tell them to say "On."

....

215 Hospital Tag

The basic rules are the same as tag. One person is "Mr. Yuck" and the others run. When you get tagged, you are "wounded" by Mr. Yuck and cover your wound with one of your hands. When you get tagged a second time, you cover your wound with your other hand. The third time you get tagged, you are out.

216 Alphabet Signs

In this car game, the object is to read out all the letters of the alphabet, in order. You can only read the next letter when you see a road sign on your side of the road. The first person to reach Z wins.

217 The Cow Game

This is a car game. You keep a count of all the cows you pass on your side of the road, but every time you pass a cemetery, you lose all your points. The winner at the end of the day's journey gets a treat!

218 My Father Owns a Grocery Store

In this car game, one player begins the round by saying: "*My father owns a grocery store, and in it he sells...*"— completing the sentence with something that begins with the letter A, such as "*apples.*"

The next player says: "*My father owns a grocery store, and in it he sells apples and...*"— something that begins with B, e.g. "*bananas.*" Each new player has to recite the entire list and add a new entry for the next letter of the alphabet.

If someone misses an item, they're supposed to be out, but give them clues to keep the game going. It makes the drive more fun.

219 Over the Mountain

Pile up soft pillows to create a mountain for toddlers to climb. They will spend a lot of time climbing up and rolling down. Invite them to move the pillows to another corner of the room and build their own mountain.

220 Makeshift Trampoline

Who says you need a massive outdoor space for a trampoline? Make your own inside by covering an old crib mattress with a crib sheet. Make sure nothing is nearby to fall against. Bouncing is sheer joy to a toddler.

221 Glove Puppets

You can find glove puppets in stores or easily make your own. Many stores sell glove puppets in the form of animals. Children love putting these on their hands and playing with them, and they stay on better than hand puppets.

To make your own glove puppets, just use a pair of old gloves. You can treat them like finger puppets, and draw faces and hair on each finger, or you can use the fingers of the glove like feet.

★ The puppets can be big or small depending on the size of glove you use.

222 Hot Potato

All the children stand in a circle and pass a beanbag around the circle to music. When the music stops, the child holding the beanbag is out. Pretend the beanbag is a very, very, very HOT POTATO!

223 The Knot

All the children form a close circle. Then everybody reaches out and holds the hands of two other children. Now, they must try to untangle the "knot" without letting go. They may have to climb over arms or crawl under arms. It helps to be supple!

224 I Spy

In this game, one child is "King Bee." The King Bee picks an object he can see. He can only say the color of the object in the following rhyme:

Bumble Bee! Bumble Bee!
I see something you don't see
and the color of it is (red).

The other "bees" (players) try to guess the object until someone figures out what it is. The bee with the right answer becomes King Bee for the next round.

225 Milk Carton City

This has been a favorite of our children for years!

For this game, save cardboard milk cartons or cereal boxes. Wash them out, cut off the tops, and then place two cartons or boxes together to form a block. You can do this with various sizes of milk cartons.

When you have at least 20 blocks, you can build a city with them. Toddlers love to see a tall tower of milk carton blocks and run over to knock them down!

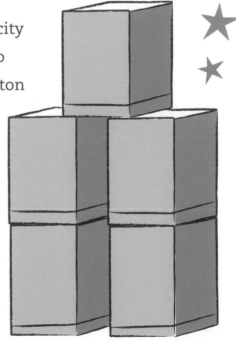

Music &
Role Play

226 Cup Game

The cup game is a rhythm game played with plastic cups. Get the children to play a beat with their hands and their cup as they sing a song. At the end of the song, they pass their cup to the person to their right and start over again, getting faster and faster and faster.

227 Animal Disco

Line up a variety of different tunes for your children to listen to—fast, slow, classical, pop, rock 'n' roll and so on. Ask them to choose an animal to go with the music and let them act out their movements. For example, they could pretend to be snake slithering along to a slow song, or rabbits hopping in time to fast pop tune.

3+ 1+ 20 *

228 Little Drummer

Use a drum if you have one; if not, turn a bowl upside down. Tap a tune on your drum or bowl. Start simply, with just one pat. Have your preschooler repeat your tune. Each time he follows you successfully, make your next tune a little bit harder.

Try this pattern:

★ One pat with your left hand.

★ Two pats with your left hand.

★ Two pats with your left hand, one pat with your right.

★ Two pats with your left hand, two pats with your right...

See how far you can get!

229 Drawing to Music

You Need: ★ A large sheet of paper ★ Crayons, pens, and pencils ★ Several different kinds of music, both fast and slow

Play the music and encourage the children to draw while listening to the different tempos. They don't need to make a picture, just move their hands to the rhythm of the music and see what comes out.

For older kids, who might be worried about what their picture looks like, encourage them to close their eyes or blindfold them so they truly just draw what they hear.

230 Blow Your Own Horn

Make a "woodwind" instrument by blowing across the
top of a bottle. Experiment with various sizes of bottles.
You'll discover that larger bottles make a lower sound
than smaller bottles when you blow across them.

231 A Saxophone of Your Own

Hold a small pocket comb with the teeth toward you.
Place a small piece of paper on the comb on the side
closest to you, holding it in place with your thumbs.
By holding the comb and paper together with your lips
and blowing, you can make the paper play a tune.

232 A Trumpet Length...

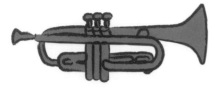

Fact: When uncoiled, a trumpet is six feet long.

Look at a photo of a trumpet, and give the children the above fact. Using a measuring tape, ask them to figure out how many trumpet lengths make up the dining table. For example, "My table is two trumpets (12 feet) long."

Then ask them to work out how many trumpets it would take to walk from their bedroom to the kitchen. What about the backyard? How many trumpets would it take to go from home to their school? What other items or distances can you measure using a trumpet?

233 Shake Your Maracas

Collect two small, plastic bottles, uncooked rice, pasta, or dried beans, and some masking tape. Partially fill the bottles with the rice, pasta, or beans. Tape over the tops of the bottles and you have two maracas to shake!

234 What Do You Hear?

Ask the children to close their eyes, be absolutely silent for a minute, and listen for any sounds they can hear. Use a kitchen timer. When the bell rings, the kids can yell out what they heard: "I heard the table creak and I heard somebody breathing!" Talk about where the sounds were coming from and how sounds can be found in almost everything around you.

235 Sound Safari

Ask your kids if they want to make some noise. Tell them they are going on a "Sound Safari" where they should make as many different sounds as they can (but not hit anything too hard, especially glass). Then let them loose!

They could bang on everything in sight with chopsticks or a whisk. Pots can become gongs, cabinet doors become drums, and pot lids become cymbals. They might make shakers out of a box of salt or canisters of dried beans.

★ To make things really interesting, start a guessing game. Close your eyes while the kids clang different objects and strikers.

236 Hide a Song

Fill three glasses with varying amounts of water. You should be able to pick out "Twinkle Twinkle Little Star" or "Mary Had a Little Lamb" by tapping a spoon on them. Tell the children you have a song hidden somewhere in the room. See if they can figure out where.

....

237 Good Vibrations

Put your child's hands lightly on your throat and hum loudly. Ask: *"What do you feel?"* Explain that the word "vibrate" means to move up and down, or back and forth rapidly, and that our vocal cords do that in order to make sounds that we form into words.

238 A Ripple in the Water

Fill a glass bowl with water and put it on a table. When the water becomes still, drop a coin in. Point out the ripples to your child. Explain that when someone speaks or makes a sound, the air ripples or vibrates, and our ears collect the sound vibrations so we hear the sound.

239 Other Vibrations

Hold one end of a plastic ruler flat against a desk and pluck the other end. Make a vibrating string instrument by stretching rubber bands over empty tissue boxes. Pluck the rubber bands where the opening is and you have your own miniature guitar.

240 String Violin

Bend up the bottom of a clothes hanger, so that the hanger forms a shape like an upside-down smile. Tie a length of string between the two bottom corners, and pull it tight so that the string is taut.

Take a second length of string about 3 feet long and tie one end of it to something solid. Pull the other end tight with your hand and "play" it by plucking it. Now pull your clothes hanger "bow" across the string, and play it like a giant violin.

241 Karaoke

No, you don't need a microphone and a television that shows you the words. Little ones love to sing—so play some tunes on your CD player and give them a hairbrush to sing into! Even if you don't know the words, pretending to be a rock star is great fun.

242 Coffee Can Drums

Grab a couple of coffee cans with plastic lids and a couple of wooden spoons for sticks. You could decorate the coffee cans with a collage of colored paper or pictures cut out of magazines.

243 Tin Can Telephone

Punch a small hole in the bottom of two cans. From the outside, insert one end of a piece of string into the hole in one can. Tie a couple of knots in the end so the string will not slip back through when pulled tight. Do the same with the other end of the string and the other can.

With one child holding each can, stretch the string so that it is tight. If one child talks into a can, it sends vibrations through the tightened string to the other can. The child with their ear to the other can will be able to hear what the first child is saying.

244 Flowerpot Chimes

You Need: ★ Four clay flowerpots in a variety of small sizes ★ A wooden dowel rod ★ String

Cut four lengths of string—30, 24, 18, and 12 inches long. The largest pot should be with the longest string. Put one end of the string through each pot's hole and knot it inside so the pot hangs upside down from the string. Now tie the free end of the string to the dowel rod, arranging the pots from largest to smallest.

Hold the rod so the pots hang freely while the children strike the pots gently with a wooden spoon to produce sound.

245 Kids Through History

Find paintings and photographs of children from various periods of history. Compare them with photographs of children today. Notice the different clothing, backgrounds, and other details. Now ask your child to paint a self-portrait modeled on an old portrait. If they would like, they could include modern details in the background, such as a videogame console.

246 Art Critics

Put a famous print up on the wall for a week. Tell your children who the artist is and why and how they made their picture. Discuss the picture and brainstorm ideas about it. You could look at a book about the artist, too.

247 Coffee Table Art

Keep a large book of art on the coffee table. Your kids will naturally flick through it and learn something. Change the book every week or two to keep it fresh. If you choose grown-ups' books, do go through them to make sure all the works are appropriate for your family.

248 Painting Sense

Look at a painting and talk about the senses. One favorite is Rousseau's "The Sleeping Gypsy" (1897). There is sight (the moonlight night), smell (lion sniffing), hearing (the mandolin), taste (water in the vase), and touch (the texture of clothing). Try other paintings, too.

249 Cave Art

Explain to the children that the oldest art was found in caves. Make cave drawings by cutting apart a brown paper bag and crumpling it to imitate a rock wall. Use oil pastels to outline the shapes you see formed by the wrinkles, and crayons to color them in.

250 What If...?

Ask each other "What if?" questions. For younger children, ask questions such as *"What if a lion squeaked instead of roared?"* or *"What if people lived in the water?"* Older children might like *"What if gravity pulled us away from the Earth instead of toward it?"* or *"What if Columbus had sailed right past America?"*

251 Reading With a Twist

Read a story with your child. Ask what is happening in the pictures, or ask your child to make up a new story based on one of the illustrations. Children can also be encouraged to think up a new ending to a story, or to tell the full story of a minor character.

252 Act It Out!

Storytelling really brings out the imagination in children. Ask your children to act out a story you tell, or reverse it, and ask your kids to act and you or other children make up a story to tell from the "scene."

253 Tell a Story

Encourage children to tell stories out loud to you or a group of other kids. You can also have each child tell part of a story and then move on to the next child, or alternate by sentence. Get them started by providing the first few sentences yourself.

254 Act Out Simple Stories

Use toys and stuffed animals to act out stories such as "Goldilocks and the Three Bears." Act out other stories by asking your toddler to play a part. Most children love being the Gingerbread Man and getting chased. This activity teaches children that the ideas we read about can enrich our lives.

255 Toddler Newspaper

All toddlers want to be like Mom and Dad, so here's a chance for them to pretend they are adults.

Take an old section of the newspaper and tape pictures of animals to the pages. Now sit down on the floor with your toddler and start to pretend to read the newspaper. Ask her to turn the next page and act surprised when you see the animals. Ask her the names of the animals and if she thinks there are any more.

★ Continue to look through the paper and talk about the animals or any other pictures that you see.

A doggie!

256 Pretend Reading

When your child has heard a book several times, ask him if he would like to "read" it to you or to someone else. Many

toddlers like to pretend to read to their dolls and stuffed animals when they put them to bed.

257 Alphabet Dress

Sing and say rhymes to your child while you are changing diapers, dressing, or washing your hands. Try the alphabet song: *"Let's sing the alphabet song while we get dressed. I wonder what letter we will get up to."*

258 Ask For Help

Ask your child to help you find a particular food in the grocery store flyer or on the store shelf: "*Can you help me see where the fruits are?*" or "*Can you find the box of...?*" (insert your child's favorite cereal).

259 Public Signs

Ask your child to help you read public print. You can say something like this: "*Will you help Mommy look for the 'Stop' signs? I don't want to miss them!*"

260 In the Paper

Ask your child to help you find parts of the newspaper: the weather report, TV guide, sports scores, and movies. Point to some of the words or letters and tell your child what they say.

261 Scribbles

It's time to scribble! Give your toddler some paper and crayons, and let them scribble away. Young toddlers love to see what kind of marks they can make. Talk to your toddler about the scribbles:

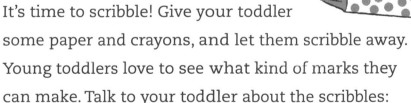

"You made a line and a dot. This line is thicker than that one. You used two colors, red and blue."

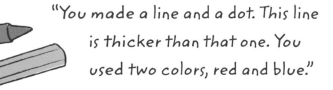

262 Copycat Scribble

Draw a line or shape and then let your child trace it or draw next to it. Take it in turns to scribble and copy, playing with line, color, and shape.

263 Draw a Scene

Make simple pictures that are related to stories you read together: scribble a forest for the three bears to go walking in, paint a pool of water for a frog to swim in, or color a mud puddle for a pig to wallow in.

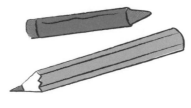

264 Faces

Make pictures of your child's favorite people or animals. Make a simple face with eyes, nose, and mouth. Use straight lines for arms and legs.

265 Felt Feelings

Buy some different colored sheets of felt and cut out circles to make faces, eyes, and noses. Cut out different mouth shapes to show feelings (happy, sad, etc.). Create a face board and use the different faces to show happy, sad, mad, scared, and other feelings. Felt works well because it sticks and is easy to get off and on quickly.

266 Signed By A Star

Print your child's name at the bottom of her drawings and say that now everyone will know who made them. Over time, guide your child (hand over hand) in printing her name herself. Be sure to make large, simple letters so that your child can see them clearly.

267 Write It Up

Let your child join you as you write. Let him sign his name to greeting cards, or write on your grocery list: *"Make two lines here to remind Mommy that we need two boxes of cereal."*

268 Past and Future

Young toddlers tend to talk about the present: "Me want cookie." Help your toddler learn new words to talk about what he or she did in the past and will do in the future. *"Yesterday you went down the slide at the park." "Tomorrow we're going to the store."*

269 Going Over the Day

Talk with your toddler about what happened during the day: *"You had a busy day today. This morning, you and Sam played in the sprinkler. You ate a peanut butter sandwich for lunch. After your nap we visited Poppy. What else did we do?"*

270 Simple Directions

Most toddlers understand more words than they are able to say. Give your toddler simple directions and give praise for following them: *"Please go to the bathroom and get your hairbrush." "Great! You got the brush. Now you can brush your hair."*

271 Role Play

Play make-believe with your toddler. You can pretend to talk on the phone, feed a doll or stuffed animal, or go shopping. Talk while you play, and encourage your toddler to talk back. Initiate conversations, for example: *"Brring, Brring. Hello. Yes, Jack is here. Would you like to talk to him? Okay, I'll give him the phone."*

272 Prop It Up

Offer props such as a doctor's kit to help your toddler talk about her fears. She can be the doctor, while you are the patient. *"Oh good! That shot only hurt a little."*

....

273 Silly Rhymes

Say silly rhymes, such as *"The bed is on her head."* Make up nonsense words, like *"It's time to skidaddle to bed."* Add a new verse to a song: *"And on his farm he had a pickle...."*

274 Silly Questions

Ask your toddler silly questions to which the answer is "No"—one of every toddler's favorite words! *"Do puppies wear pajamas?" "Is the sky green?"*

275 Special Time

Have a special time for reading with your toddler every day. Some families read after dinner or as part of their bedtime routine. Toddlers may want to read a favorite book again and again, because they love the story and love feeling close to you. When they get older, they will have new favorites.

276 Just Because You Asked

Read when your toddler asks you to, so that your toddler will know that you think reading is important. If you can't stop what you are doing, suggest that the child look at a book alone for a while or ask another family member to read to the child.

277 Going To The Library

Take your toddler to the library and let her pick out her own books. Introduce your child to the librarian and participate in storytimes so the library becomes a familiar, fun place.

278 Touch and Feel

Look for books that let your toddler do something, such as touch and feel the pictures. Some books can be scratched and sniffed, or squeezed to make noises. Some books have pull-tabs that make things pop up or move to reveal hidden pictures. Books like these may wear out before your toddler gets tired of reading them.

279 Rhyme and Remember

Choose books with repeated words, rhymes, and phrases that your toddler can remember. If you read these books again and again, the child might join in at the right time and feel that he or she is reading too.

280 Questions, Questions

Ask your toddler questions about the pictures in a book. *"Who's that?"* *"Where do you think he's going?"* *"What noise do cows make?"* Ask your toddler to point to people and objects in the pictures. *"Where's the...?"*

281 Book Care

Help your toddler learn to care for books. Show your child how to turn the pages so they won't tear. Remind your child to put books away after reading them. Some well-loved books will wear out. Ask your toddler to help you fix his damaged books. Your child can show you which pages are torn.

282 Almost-Sleepover

Why not host an "almost-sleepover" for your child? It's all the fun of a sleepover without actually sleeping over!

Choose an evening when your child doesn't have to get up early the next day to host your almost-sleepover, and limit the number of guests to four or five to keep activities and socializing running smoothly. Of course, there's a dress code for the almost-sleepover: guests must come dressed in their favorite pajamas and slippers, with sleeping bags and pillows in tow.

★ This is good practice for a first real sleepover.

283 Pajama Fashion Show

A pajama fashion show is a must at an almost-sleepover. Throw some music on the CD player and give each guest the chance to strut their stuff. And don't forget to take lots of photos!

284 Decorate Pillow Cases

Why not decorate pillowcases at your almost-sleepover? Buy some inexpensive, white pillowcases and fabric markers. With a fabric marker, write each guest's name in large letters in the middle of the pillowcase, and then let them decorate their pillowcase with the markers however they choose.

285 Circle Hunt Collage

Take your toddler on an adventurous hunt through old magazines for circle shapes. After the hunt, cut out the circles and use them to create a creative circle collage. Hang your completed circle collage on the wall or refrigerator, so your toddler can look at it often, reinforcing his ability to recognize circle shapes.

286 Plan Your Day

Plan your day so there's time for your toddler to wash, dress, and feed him or herself. Your child may take longer to put on sneakers than you do, but "Me do it!" is a mark of pride.

287 Fast and Slow

Sometimes kids move at the speed of light. Other times, they're as slow as a snail. Even so, younger toddlers may be unsure exactly what the concepts "fast" and "slow" actually mean.

Play a fast song and show your toddler how to dance fast. You could say: *"This is a fast song. Move your arms and feet fast."* Then play a slow song and show your child how to dance slowly.

Repeat fast and slow songs, allowing your child to dance for as long as he or she likes.

288 Left and Right

Using a washable marker, write the letter L on your child's left hand. Make sure the letter is right side up from your child's point of view. Do the same with the letter R on your child's right hand.

For a week or so, help your child be aware of his or her actions regarding left and right. For example, when he or she picks something up, ask what hand (left or right) is used. If your child kicks a ball, ask what foot is being used to kick it.

289 Imagination Math

Imagination activities don't have to be limited to the arts. Math can be imaginative by simply guessing how many items would fill up a container, or figuring out the length of a hallway, or how many kids would fit in your living room!

290 Point It Out

Point to written words around you and read them out loud to your toddler. *"Here comes our bus. It says 'Northside' on the front. That's where we're going."* *"These diapers are too small. We need a box that says 'over 30 pounds.'"*

291 Other Reading Fun

On car trips, make it a game to point out and read license plates, billboards, and interesting road signs. Swap evening television for a good action story or tale of adventure.

. . . .

292 Look and Listen

Too tired to read aloud? Listen to a book on tape or CD, and turn the book's pages with your children. You'll still be reading with them!

293 Labels Labels Labels

Label things in your children's room as they learn to name them. Have fun while they learn that written words are connected to everyday things.

294 Pack It!

Pack a snack, pack a book! Going someplace where there might be a long wait? Bring along a snack and a bag of your child's favorite books.

295 Recipe for Reading

The next time you cook with your children, read the recipe with them. Step-by-step instructions, ingredients, and measurements are all part of words in print!

296 Another Language

Learning a foreign language by listening to tapes can be boring, but listening to stories, folk tales, rhymes, and songs on tape in another language is great fun! Find a picture dictionary of the foreign language you've chosen and try to pick out the words you hear.

297 Make a Book

Reading becomes more interesting when a toddler learns how a book is made.

Help your child write out a story he or she thinks of, or type it out if you have a computer. Then, show your child how to illustrate the story with pictures, make a cover, and put it all together. You can do this simply by stapling the pages together or putting some holes in the side and tying it with a ribbon.

You can make books for all kinds of things: letter and number books, scrapbooks, animal identification—you name it!

298 A Reading Pocket

Slip fun things to read into your pocket to bring home:
a comic strip from the paper, a greeting card, or even
a fortune cookie from lunch. Create a special, shared
moment your child can look forward to every day.

299 Such a Cliché

It's as black as night, as wet as water, or as sticky as
syrup! Once your child starts to "get" synonyms (and
all the other "nyms"), finding clichés becomes a game.
When you hear one, say, *"That's such a cliché!"* You can
make a great car game by making them up.

300 Water the Plants

Collect some bath toys that you fill up with water and squirt. Put some plants on the porch or in the sink and let your toddler use his water squirter to water the plants. While watering the plants you can talk about the leaves, flowers, and other plant words.

....

301 Indoor Pond

Place some play sand in a large bucket. In the middle of the bucket, dig a hole in the sand large enough for a plastic tub to fit in, and fill it with water. Place toy frogs and fish around the sand and in the water, and let the children explore your indoor pond!

302 Row Your Boat

Partner up the children (or family members) and, sitting on the floor, show them how to rock back and forth as if rowing a boat. Sing the song "Row, Row, Row Your Boat." The children will initiate this activity on their own when they get to know the song and motion.

303 Row It Again

Get a large or medium-sized plastic boat. While singing the song "Row, Row, Row Your Boat," one toddler holds the boat and rocks it back and forth. At the end of the song, it is someone else's turn and the boat must be passed to the next person.

Solo Adventures

304 Garden Art

Find pictures of flowers, insects, birds, and grass in magazines, and cut them out. On a large piece of white paper, let your toddler create his own garden with the flowers and glue. When the flowers are in place, you can put a strip of grass along the bottom. Then add the insects and birds, and you're there!

305 This belongs to: ...ME!

Let your toddler draw on a sheet of printable labels using colored crayons or pencils. Then print her name, or "This belongs to" on the labels. Put the labels on toys, lunch bags, backpacks, books, clothes, or other things that your toddler wants to identify as "Mine!"

306 Pizza Chefs

Cut a yellow (crust) piece of felt into a circle, about eight inches in diameter. Then cut a red piece of felt into a circle about six inches in diameter. Now cut the red circle in half, and the halves into three wedges each (like pizza slices.)

Use other pieces of felt to create the toppings:
* ★ Black for olives (small squares)
* ★ Green for green peppers
* ★ White for cheese (strips)
* ★ Dark red for pepperoni (circles)

Now let your toddler put the pizza together. First lay down the yellow circle, add the slices of red felt on top, and add all the toppings as you please!

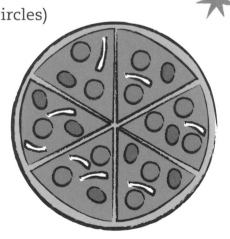

307 The Pizza Game

You Need: ★ Paper plates ★ Glue ★ Colored paper ★ Scissors

Take some paper plates and color the rim light brown and the middle orangey-red. These are your "pizzas."

Next, take some colored paper and cut out lots of "toppings," such as mushrooms, pepperoni slices, and olives. Glue a few pieces of each topping on each of your pizzas. Use a different number of each topping—such as four olives, five anchovies, and six mushrooms.

On a piece of paper, make a simple topping table with a row for each topping. Stick one piece of each topping to the left of each row.

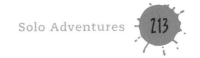

308 Toddler Jump Rope!

It's time to have some fun and jump rope... well, maybe just some string. This is an activity that you can do indoors or outdoors.

Lay a rope in a zigzag pattern in the grass or on your floor. Challenge your child to walk on the rope, or along the zigzags. Then lay it straight and have your child walk the tightrope—arms outstretched. You could even ask your child to perform various circus-type tricks on it—somersaults, jumps, twists and the like! Then have your child think of ways to jump over it, under it, or whatever! You'll be surprised at how creative they become.

309 Handy Colors

Using some latex gloves, paint the fingers of both gloves red, yellow, blue, green and orange, so that you have two of each color. Then sing this song to the tune of "Are You Sleeping?":

Where is red?
(bring one hand up with all the fingers showing)
Where is red? (repeat with the other hand)
Here I am, (wave one hand)
Here I am. (wave the other hand)
Show me if you can, (hold both hands up)
Show me if you can.
Where is red?
Where is red?

Repeat this with all the colors, allowing your toddler to show you the colors.

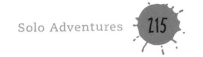

310 Upside-down Art

Tape white paper under a table. Give the children a theme for their artwork. Then give them chalk, markers, crayons, or pastels to do their artwork under the table while lying on the floor.

311 Backward Day

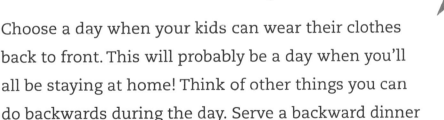

Choose a day when your kids can wear their clothes back to front. This will probably be a day when you'll all be staying at home! Think of other things you can do backwards during the day. Serve a backward dinner to finish the day. Start with dessert, followed by the main course, and the salad and veggies last if the kids have any room left.

312 Treasure Map

Help your children draw a map of the yard and tell them that it's a treasure map. They can look out of the window or go outside to check what it looks like. Help them to draw a key that shows rocks, bushes, and other details.

Now give the children some type of treasure, like quarters or chocolate coins, and ask them to put it somewhere in the yard. Then ask them how they would give directions on how to find the treasure from your back door. They can use the number of paces (steps), and the words "left" and "right."

313 Box Fort

You Need: ★ Large packing boxes ★ Scissors
★ Scotch tape ★ Markers for decorating the fort

Ask your kids how they want their fort to look. What
type of windows? Windows that open up, open down,
or open out? Carefully cut out each window opening,
leaving a flap (or two flaps) to be opened and closed.
Then cut out a door in the same place in each box,
so it's possible to walk from one box to another.
Now tape the boxes together, making sure that you
line up the door openings. Draw in the details.

314 Dough Art

Defrost some frozen dough in a large greased bowl covered with a towel, to prevent it from drying out.

When the dough has risen, punch down and separate into large chunks for each child. Give them aprons, a lightly floured work area, and a blunt knife. Ask them to make animals, plants, or objects that interest them out of the dough. Place the dough shapes on a greased cookie sheet, then paint them with food coloring mixed with a little bit of water.

Leave the cookies for one to two hours. Then bake them in the oven for about 20–30 minutes at 350°F.

315 Under the Table

Plan a fun meal, like taco salad or another food that everyone puts together themselves. Pull away all the chairs and sit cross-legged under the table. Warning: the children will enjoy this so much that they will bug you until you do it again!

....

316 Washing Up

Summer is an ideal time to wash all the grime off your toys (or your car), and we all know how young children like to help. So bring out bowls of soapy water, dishcloths, tea towels, and aprons—and get washing!

317 Fall Leaf Book

Take the kids out on a fall leaf hunt. Help them to collect fallen leaves of as many different colors and shapes as possible.

Cut sheets of clear contact paper into uniform pieces. Peel back half of the protective paper and place one or more leaves on the exposed side. Then peel back the rest of the paper and fold back over the other side to seal. When all the leaves are sealed, use strips of construction

paper to frame each leaf page. Punch a hole through the corner of each completed page and tie with a piece of string to form a book.

 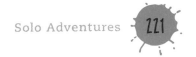

318 Spot the Button

Cut some miniature shirts out of card. Sew, or stick using craft glue, four buttons on each shirt. Three of the buttons should be identical, and the fourth just a little different in size, color, style, or number of holes. Make lots of different shirts.

Your child has to spot the different button by placing a ring around it. You can buy plastic rings in craft departments, or use the rings left on juice or milk bottles when you first unscrew the lid.

319 Bubble Fun

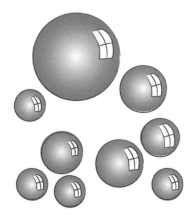

Fill a dishpan with dishwashing liquid and water. Add a little corn syrup or glycerin to give the bubbles more staying power.

Now send your child on a bubble-blower scavenger hunt. Anything that is water resistant, has one or more holes, and will fit in the dishpan is a bubble blower. Slotted spoons, spatulas, fly swatters, potato mashers, short lengths of PVC pipe, and keys—there's no end to the bubble blowers you can find in your home! Now let your child dip the blower in and blow some bubbles!

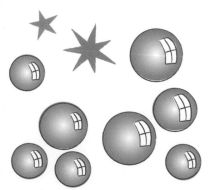

Try setting up a target near the pan of bubbles and see if your child can blow the bubbles toward the target.

320 Catch a Capital

Cut out some little paper baseball mitts and write a lower-case letter on each one. Now cut out the same number of baseballs and write a capital letter on each one. Have your child match the baseball capital with the lower-case mitt.

· ·

321 Comic Strip Creator

Give your kids a theme for a story. Then have them go through magazines and newspapers looking for interesting things to cut out. Lay the pieces out on plain paper and glue them in order of the story, leaving room for the writing below. Now have them write the story out below the pictures.

322 The Flower Shop

Get some old plastic vases and fake flowers from garage sales or thrift stores. Now put the scratch side of a Velcro dot on the front of each vase. Put the soft side of the Velcro on small squares of card, and write different numbers on the cards, from one to ten, depending how many flowers you have.

Place a different card on the front of each vase and have your child put the correct number of flowers in the vase. If you write colors on the cards instead of numbers, it's a sorting game instead.

323 Felt Fun

Make a felt board by wrapping a piece of felt around a sturdy piece of plywood, cardboard, or posterboard. Secure all the edges around the back with duct tape, staples, or tacks.

Using scrap pieces of felt or fabric squares, start by cutting out different shapes and sticking them on the board. Then try numbers, letters, and animals. You can also color images from coloring books or use pictures from magazines. Just mount these on some card, and glue some small squares of sandpaper or Velcro to the back so that it will stick to the felt board.

324 Cork Drumsticks

Take two corks. With a sharp pencil, start a hole in the center of one side of each cork. Finish the holes with chopsticks. Fill the hole with a small amount of glue and insert the chopsticks, allowing them to dry before use. Now find a drum!

325 Cylinder Drum

Find a cylindrical metal cookie or chips container. Remove and throw away the lid. Cut out a piece of fabric large enough to fit over the container and overlap the edges by one and a half inches.

Cover the container and secure the fabric tightly using rubber bands.

 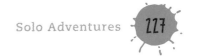

326 Make Music! ★

Cut some waxed paper to fit over one end of a paper towel tube. Secure the paper with several rubber bands. Poke a few holes in the waxed paper and hum into the unpapered end to make music!

....

327 Lid Sort

Collect a variety of plastic containers and their detached lids. Your toddler can find and put the matching lid on each container. Cleaned and dried plastic bottles such as those used for shampoo or mustard have distinctive lids that are easy to match and attach.

328 Find the Sock

Gather up your unpaired socks fresh from the laundry. Ask your toddler to separate the dark colors from the light ones, then see if he can match up the pairs. Later, he can sort the clothes by category (for example, shirts in one spot and pants in another).

329 Table Dressing

Set a place at the table with a fork, spoon, cup, and napkin in front of a chair. Put more forks, spoons, cups, and napkins in the middle of the table and let your toddler copy your place setting in front of the other chairs.

330 Dishwasher Stacker

Show your child where the cups and plates go in the dishwasher, and where you put the forks and spoons. Now pass your child a dirty item (not glasses or knives) and see if she can find the right place for it.

331 Making the Bed

Show your child how to bring up a corner, press down wrinkles, and tuck in unseemly overhangs. Then let him do the same on the next bed you make. Let him arrange the pillows—and when you walk through the bedroom later, those crooked pillows will make you smile!

332 Fun with Dusting

Feather dusters tickle, they're funny looking, and they work! Give your child a feather duster, tell her which areas need cleaning and any that are off-limits, and remove any breakable items from surfaces. Then let her get to work!

333 Sweeping and Vacuuming

Show your child how to use a hand-held vacuum, a lightweight rechargeable upright, or a carpet sweeper. You can sweep the dirt into piles and let him watch with satisfaction as they magic the dirt away.

334 Sorting Cereal

Put your toddler in a high chair and provide a few handfuls of colored cereal loops and a muffin pan. With a little direction, she will sort the cereal by color into the muffin pan cups (and enjoy a little snack in the process).

335 Tasty Art

Gather a bowl of diced fruit with a little peanut butter and some crackers. First, thinly spread the peanut butter on the crackers. Then let your toddler press fruit chunks into the peanut butter to create nutritious works of art. Your toddler could be the next Picasso!

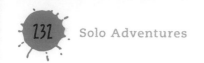

336 Flower Power

Half-fill six glasses with cool water. Color the water in each glass a different color using food coloring. Place a carnation in each glass. When they have changed color, make a nice bouquet of "homemade" colorful carnations to display around the house.

337 Theme Baths

Turn your kids' bath into the sea by adding a drop of blue food coloring and giving them different sea-creature toys to play with. Or use green food coloring to make it into a jungle swamp and give them toy crocodiles to lurk in the shallows.

338 Float or Sink?

At your child's bath time, gather together objects of different weights, like plastic ducks, coins, a ping-pong ball, and metal spoons. Before you drop each object in the bath, ask your child to guess whether it will float or sink. Then find out if he or she was right!

339 Liquid Layers

Pour ⅓ cup of syrup, then ⅓ cup of cooking oil, and finally ⅓ cup of water into a jar. Let the liquids settle for a few minutes. Drop a plastic button, a grape, and a small cork into the liquid one at a time. Try to guess in advance which object will settle in which layer of liquid.

340 Electrifying Fun

Cut a piece of string approximately 12–16 inches long. Tie a piece of O-shaped cereal to one end of the string, and tie the other end to the edge of a table.

Wash a comb with hot soapy water and dry it completely. Run the comb through long, dry hair about ten times, or rub the comb quickly on a woolly sweater. The comb will now be charged.

Slowly bring the comb toward the piece of cereal and stop as soon as you see the cereal swing toward and touch the comb. Keep the comb still and wait until the cereal moves away by itself. Now move the comb toward the piece of cereal again. This time, the cereal should move away.

341 Windowsill Garden

When snowdrifts keep your kids inside, try cultivating a windowsill garden. All you need is a sunny spot, a few containers of soil, and some pot-loving plants. Herbs are an excellent choice for windowsills.

....

342 Peculiar Plants

What kid wouldn't be fascinated by an insect-eating plant? Buy a Venus flytrap from your nearest garden center. Then put a dead fly on the "trap" ends of one of the leaves and watch the trap shut fast!

343 Sprouting Seeds

Line a glass jar with a damp paper towel and put several zucchini seeds between the glass and the towel. Place a lid on the jar, leave it on the kitchen counter, and check the paper every day to make sure it's still moist. Watch how the seeds sprout in a few days' time.

344 Gardening Club

Join the kids' gardening club at your nearest garden center and find out about any special workshops they run, such as building a birdhouse.

345 Decorate While You Wait

Let your kids indulge their natural creativity by painting inexpensive terra cotta pots to use next spring, for repotting houseplants this winter, or for gifts. Kid-safe, durable paints can be bought at most craft stores.

346 Seed Planning

Show your child a gardening book and let him help you plan which plants to grow from seed. Then let him choose some varieties from some seed catalogs, or help you choose them at the garden center. Ask the experts at your garden center when to start the seeds.

347 Glass Garden

Carefully place some soil, a few mosses, and some plants (with roots) inside a clean mayonnaise jar. Keep your indoor garden moist with a plant mister, and cover the opening with clear plastic wrap.

348 Plant Markers

Collect some popsicle sticks or small wooden stakes (dowels work great, too). Cut them, if you need to, into uniform lengths. Write the names of your plants on them with permanent marker, then hand the sticks over to your child to decorate. They can be painted, drawn on, or sprinkled with glue and glitter.

349 Fly Away Bird

You Need: ★ Old CDs or DVDs, or shiny cans ★ Streamers ★ String

This is a great way to keep birds out of the garden. Take leftover cans or scratched CDs and DVDs, and glue or tape streamers to them. Then tie a string to each one and tie them to a tree or a fence around your garden. Not only do they shine in the sun, they blow in the wind as well, making your garden look pretty. They also give a fright to deer and birds, keeping your plantings safe!

350 Fishing Fun

Draw or print out pictures of fish and other sea creatures, then cut out and attach paper clips or washers. Make a pole by tying a length of string to the end of a pencil and glue a magnet to the other end of the string. Make a tape of yourself giving your child directions so that she can do this activity on her own.

351 Silly Walks

Ask your child to walk around in her normal, everyday walk. Now try walking very high, very low, very wide, very narrow, very fast, and very slowly. Now ask your child to create her own special walk and make it as silly as possible—backward, sideways, or turning.

352 Bead Patterns

For this you will need medium-large beads and thin,
round shoelaces. Create up to ten bead patterns on a
length of string or yarn. Tie off each end so the beads
don't fall off. Include more lengths of yarn along with
the beads for the child to copy your bead patterns.

353 Rainy Day

On a rainy day put a few lines or circles of different
colors of paint onto a big poster board. Set it outside
and have the your toddler watch what the rain does to
the paint. After a few minutes (depending how hard it is
raining out) bring the it back inside and ask your her to
tell you which pictures she can find in the painting.

354 Build-a-meal

For this you will need a sturdy paper plate, Velcro, and pictures of food. Place one side of several Velcro dots on the paper plate and the other sides on the back of your food pictures. Have your child create healthy meals for his or her stuffed animals or action figures!

355 Road Map

On squares of card, draw two-inch-wide paths that start and end at the very center of each card. They can be decorated to be streets or a river—your child can use toy cars or boats to "drive" down the paths they create with their cards! Give your child stickers of street signs, trees, animals, etc. to decorate the sides of the path cards.

In the Kitchen

356 Bird's-eye View

Give each child a stable step-stool, just high enough to allow them to safely reach the counter or table. Even if there isn't actually anything for them to do, they'll love watching you cook, and it's a great opportunity to chat.

357 Dress to Chef

Before you start cooking with your child, get dressed for the job! Find a kid-sized apron, a mini chef's hat, or just one of Dad's big old shirts to get your little assistant into the mood for cooking.

358 Sort It

At the kitchen table, give your child a small muffin pan and a pile of different items, such as coins or quarters, buttons, nuts, bottle caps, paper clips, rubber bands, or bread holders. See if he can sort the items into separate cups in the muffin tin.

359 Count Them

Place muffin liners in a muffin pan and write a number from one to six on the bottom of each liner. Then give your child a pile of nuts or raisins, and have him or her place the number of items in each cup that corresponds with the number written on the liner.

360 Guesstimate...

Set out two or three small, plastic containers filled with different numbers amounts of food items, such as eight baby carrots, 12 grapes, or ten fish crackers. Have your child try to guess how many items are in each box. Next, have them empty out their box and count their snacks.

361 Big to Small

Give your child a set of measuring cups. Ask her to line them up on the table in order of size, biggest to smallest. Next, ask her to place one raisin in the smallest cup. Then ask her to place five raisins in the biggest cup, and so on. It's fun and makes great counting practice!

362 Sandwich Shapes

Ask your child if he wants you to cut his sandwich into two rectangles, two triangles, or four squares. You may need to demonstrate these shapes a few times, but sooner or later your child will become a whiz at recognizing them. He will also be learning about simple fractions.

363 Kitchen Math

Ask your child to help you get one pickle from the jar, six crackers from the package, or two big carrots from the refrigerator. The opportunities for doing math in the kitchen are endless!

364 Two for One

Ask your child: "*We have four people and eight cookies. How many cookies will each person get?*" This is a simple two-to-one relationship. Look for other opportunities for your child to learn these, and one-to-one relationships.

365 Place-setting Math

Set out a stack of napkins and have your child count out how many are needed to set the table. Do the same with cutlery (not knives) and dishes. Setting the table is a great opportunity for your child to practice counting.

3+ 1+ 50 ***

366 My First Apple Pie

You Need: ★ 1 double pie dough ★ 5 cups apple slices ★ ½ cup sugar ★ 1 tbsp all-purpose flour ★ ¼ tsp nutmeg ★ ¼ tsp allspice ★ ½ tsp cinnamon ★ Juice of half a lemon ★ 2 tbsp butter

Preheat the oven to 400°F. Line an 8-inch pie plate with pie dough and trim the edges. Combine the apple slices, sugar, flour, spices, and lemon juice in a large bowl. Spoon the mixture into the pie dough and dot with butter. Fold the top crust in half, set it over the fruit, and unfold. Seal the edges with a fork. Cut decorative slits in the crust.

Bake for 40 minutes or until your pie is bubbly and golden brown.

367 My First Cookies

You Need: ★ 3 cups white flour ★ 1½ cups whole wheat flour ★ 1 tsp salt ★ 2 tbsp baking powder ★ 1 cup butter, cut into small pieces ★ ⅔ cup milk or buttermilk

Mix the dry ingredients in a large bowl. Use a fork to  blend in the butter until the mixture looks uniformly crumbly. Stir in the milk until the mixture forms a dough. Knead it a few times. Pat or roll it out, about ½ inch thick, on a lightly floured surface. Use cookie cutters to punch out the cookies and place them on a baking sheet.

Bake at 425°F for 10–12 minutes until lightly browned.

368 Chocolate Chip Cookies

You Need: ★ 2¹/₃ cups all-purpose flour ★ 1 tsp baking powder ★ ¹/₂ tsp salt ★ 1 cup butter ★ ²/₃ cup packed brown sugar ★ ¹/₂ cup sugar ★ 1 tbsp vegetable oil ★ 1 tbsp light corn syrup ★ 1 egg ★ 2 tsp vanilla extract ★ 1 package chocolate chips ★ ³/₄ cup chopped walnuts or pecans (optional)

Preheat the oven to 350°F. Stir together the flour, baking powder, and salt. In a separate bowl, stir the butter, sugars, oil, and corn syrup. Add the egg and vanilla extract, and then the flour mixture, chocolate chips, and nuts (check for allergies before using nuts).

Drop 2 tablespoons of dough onto lightly greased baking sheets, leaving about 3 inches between the cookies. Bake for 15–18 minutes or until the cookies are lightly browned.

369 Rice Fun

Set down a container of uncooked rice along with some spoons, measuring cups, and other containers for pouring. Your toddler will have a blast feeling, pouring, and scooping the rice. It's that simple!

370 Honey Buns

You Need: ★ 1 package split hot-dog buns ★ Peanut butter ★ 2–3 bananas ★ Honey ★ Sunflower seeds

Slice the bananas and set aside. Spread the peanut butter on the buns. Put the banana slices on top. Drip with honey and sprinkle with sunflower seeds. Yummy!

371 Peanut Butter Balls

You Need: ★ ½ cup peanut butter ★ ½ cup honey ★ 1 cup crushed cornflakes ★ 2 tbsp powdered milk

Set the cornflakes aside. Mix all the other ingredients well. Roll into balls, then roll them again in the cornflakes until covered. Refrigerate any leftovers!

372 Nuts and Bolts

You Need: ★ 1 can cocktail peanuts ★ 1 package rice cereal ★ ½ package nut-shaped cereal ★ 1 package pretzel sticks ★ ½ cup peanut butter ★ ½ cup oil

Preheat the oven to 300°F. Mix the peanut butter and oil. Heat on the stove until smooth. Pour all ingredients into a roasting pan and mix well. Bake for 15–20 minutes.

373 Graveyard Ghosts

You Need: ★ 1 chocolate cake mix ★ 8 scoops vanilla ice cream ★ 16 mint cookies ★ Small candies ★ Shoestring licorice

Prepare the cake mix for cupcakes according to the instructions on the package. Pour the mixture into muffin cups so they are two-thirds full. Bake, cool completely, and remove from the pan.

Top each cake with a scoop of ice cream. Decorate to resemble a mouse, using mint cookies for the ears, and candies for the eyes, nose, and mouth. Insert licorice for the whiskers. If the ice cream has melted, place it in the freezer for ½ hour before serving.

374 Strawberry Ice

You Need: ★ 2 packages frozen sliced strawberries in syrup ★ ¾ cup lemonade

Mix the ingredients together in a blender or food processor until smooth. Turn off the blender, scrape the sides, blend again, and pour into a plastic container. Cover and freeze until serving time.

When you take it out of the freezer, if the ice is frozen hard, let it stand at room temperature for five minutes or so before serving.

375 Easy Breakfast Bars

You Need: ★ 2 cups granola ★ 2 eggs, beaten
★ A dash of vanilla for sweetening

Preheat the oven to 350°F. Combine the granola, eggs, and vanilla in a bowl. Spread into an 8-inch square pan. Bake for 15 minutes. Cut into bars; serve with honey or jelly.

376 Frozen Bananas

You Need: ★ 1 banana ★ Honey, peanut butter

Peel and cut the banana in half. Wrap it in plastic and freeze. When frozen, the banana is ready to eat, dipped in peanut butter or honey. You could also top it with shredded coconut or wheatgerm.

377 Waffle Sandwich

You Need: ★ 2 waffles, frozen or homemade
★ Peanut butter ★ Jelly

Optional ingredients: ★ Marshmallow spread, bananas, chocolate chips, honey, dried fruit…

Spread the peanut butter on one waffle, jelly on the other, and make a sandwich. Easy!

378 No-Bake Yogurt Pie

You Need: ★ 1 x 8-oz container of orange-flavored yogurt ★ 1 can whipped non-dairy topping ★ ½ can mandarin orange slices, drained and broken into pieces ★ 1 x 9-inch graham cracker pie crust

Combine the yogurt and whipped topping in a bowl, add the mandarin orange slices and stir. Spoon the mixture into the pie crust. Cover with plastic wrap and chill. You can also freeze this pie and thaw slightly before serving.

379 Melon Bowls

You Need: ★ Watermelon ★ Various other melons, such as honeydew and cantaloupe

Halve the watermelon. Let the kids scoop out the melon with a melon baller. Scoop out more melon balls from the other melons. Fill the melon "bowl" with the balls.

380 Smiley Face Sandwiches

You Need: ★ Peanut butter ★ Wheat bread
★ Raisins or chocolate chips

Spread peanut butter on a piece of wheat bread. Let your toddler make faces on the top using raisins or chocolate chips to make eyes, a nose, eyebrows, a smiley face, etc.

381 Taste Tester ★ ★

Turn your child into the taste tester for everything you eat! Ask him whether something is salty, sweet, sour, or bitter. As your child gets older, he might be able to help you figure out if a recipe needs more salt—or more sweetness!

382 Grocery Shopping

Before you go shopping, have your child make a grocery list. At the store, hand her items to put in the cart. Ask for help counting out apples and veggies. Then, as your child gets older, see if she can figure out how much something costs by its weight.

383 Summer Treat

Place ½ cup milk, 1 tablespoon sugar, and ½ teaspoon vanilla extract in a sandwich-sized ziplock bag. Seal the bag and put it inside a gallon-size ziplock bag. Add plenty of ice cubes and salt to the larger bag. Shake it for about ten minutes. This makes one serving of ice cream and is great for a hot summer day outdoor activity!

....

384 Squish

Fill a few ziplock bags halfway with whipped cream or mayonnaise. Then put those bags inside a very large ziplock bag. Let your tot push and step on the bags. The squish will be the most fun they've had in a long time. Supervision is essential when plastic bags are involved.

385 Dippers

Any of these dips taste delicious with apples, pears, bananas, peaches, or berries. Have a grown-up whisk each one together.

Vanilla Dip: ★ 2 (8-oz) packages cream cheese, softened ★ ½ cup brown sugar ★ 2 tsp vanilla extract

Exotic Fruit Dip: Combine cream cheese and crushed pineapple. This also tastes delicious when made with canned mandarin oranges instead of pineapple. Drain as much of the fruit juice as possible to avoid a runny dip.

Spicy Dip: Mix cream cheese, apple sauce, and a dash of cinnamon and brown sugar.

Keep in the refrigerator in an airtight container.

386 Baked Cheese Bites

You Need: ★ 2 cups sifted all-purpose flour
★ 1 pinch salt ★ 6 oz shredded Cheddar cheese
★ ½ cup butter, melted

Preheat the oven to 325°F. Mix together the flour and salt. Stir in the cheese and melted butter to form a firm dough.

Roll pieces of dough into ropes the diameter of a cent. Slice into ¼-inch pieces. You may need to chill the dough until firm for better rolling. Place the slices an inch apart on a large, greased cookie sheet.

Bake for 20–25 minutes until the bottoms of the "coins" are lightly toasted and the tops are firm.

387 English Muffin "Pizzas"

Spread spaghetti sauce on English muffin halves. Top with sliced olives, deli slices, vegetables, and grated mozzarella cheese. Heat in a toaster oven, or microwave until the cheese is melted.

388 Crazy Cake

You Need: ★ 2 tsp baking soda ★ 1 tsp salt ★ 2 cups sugar ★ 3 cups flour ★ 1/2 cup cocoa ★ 1 tsp vanilla ★ 2 tsp vinegar ★ 3/4 cup oil ★ 2 cups water

Preheat the oven to 350°F. Mix the dry ingredients in an 8-inch baking pan and smooth out. Using a spoon, make three large holes. Pour the vanilla in one, then the vinegar and oil. Pour water over the entire mix. Stir with a fork until well mixed. Bake for 35–40 minutes.

389 Fingerpaint It!

Fill a few bowls with whipped cream, and add a few drops of food coloring. Mix each bowl and you have some fingerpaints! Let your toddler get their hands stuck in and make handprints on the sink. A few swipes from the faucet will rinse it away afterward.

390 Pudding Paint

Cover a work surface with paper and make a pudding. Give each child their own container of

pudding, then let them use their fingers to do the rest. Talk about how it feels between their fingers, about the taste, and the smell.

391 Celery Fun

You Need: ★ Celery sticks ★ Cream cheese or peanut butter ★ Nuts, raisins, or other dried fruit

Wash and dry the celery sticks. Fill them with cream cheese or peanut butter. Let your child decorate them with the nuts or dried fruit. Serve as an afternoon snack.

392 Green Tortilla Chip

You Need: ★ 1 tbsp green food coloring ★ ¼ cup water ★ White corn tortilla shells

Mix the food coloring and water. With a pastry brush, brush the color on to the tortilla sides. Let it dry for an hour. Slice into triangles and fry in hot vegetable oil.

393 Soft Pretzels

You Need: ★ 2 16-oz loaves frozen bread dough, thawed ★ 1 egg white, slightly beaten ★ 1 tsp water ★ Coarse salt

Preheat the oven to 350°F. Separate the dough into 24 1$\frac{1}{2}$-inch balls. Roll each ball into a rope 14$\frac{1}{2}$ inches long. Have your children make pretzel shapes (letters or numerals). Put the shapes 1 inch apart on a greased cookie sheet. Let them stand for 20 minutes and brush with the combined egg white and water. Sprinkle with the salt.

Place a shallow pan containing 1 inch of boiling water on the bottom rack of the oven. Bake the pretzels on the rack above for 20 minutes or until golden brown.

394 Peppermint Ice Cream

You Need: ★ 3-lb coffee can with plastic cover ★ 1-lb coffee can with plastic cover ★ 2 cups whipping cream ★ ½ cup sugar ★ ½ tsp vanilla extract ★ ½ tsp peppermint extract ★ Red food coloring ★ Crushed peppermint stick ★ Rock salt ★ Crushed ice

Place the smaller can in the center of the larger can. Fill the smaller can with the cream, sugar, vanilla, and peppermint extract, food coloring, and peppermint stick. Layer crushed ice and rock salt around the smaller can. Cover both cans with their plastic lids. Sit on the floor and roll the cans back and forth for about 15 minutes.

395 Rice Crispy Bars

You Need: ★ 6 cups crisped rice ★ 1 bag white marshmallows ★ 3 tbsp butter or margarine

Melt the margarine in a no-stick pan and add the entire bag of marshmallows. Stir over a medium heat until the marshmallows have completely melted. Add the rice crispies and mix well.

Pour the mixture into a 9 x 13-inch pan that has been greased or sprayed with no-stick cooking spray. Use some greaseproof paper that has been sprayed with no-stick spray to spread and flatten the mixture. When completely cool, cut the mixture into squares.

396 Alphabet Spices

Arrange your spices and herbs alphabetically. Then label the first jar of each letter with a capital A, B, or C. Show them to your child and go through the alphabet from A to Z. Here's a list of a few seasonings and other items you can taste, smell, or explore together:

A—Allspice	**N**—Nutmeg
B—Basil	**O**—Oregano
C—Cinnamon	**P**—Paprika
D—Dill	**Q**—Quart
E—Egg	**R**—Rosemary
F—Fennel	**S**—Sage
G—Ginger	**T**—Thyme
H—Horseradish	**U**—Udon
I—Italian Seasoning	**V**—Vanilla
J—Jelly	**W**—Worcestershire sauce
K—Ketchup	**X**—Xanthan gum
L—Lemon	**Y**—Yeast
M—Mint	**Z**—Zest

397 Secret Messages

Write secret messages to your child using a toothpick or Q-tip dipped in lemon juice. Hold the paper carefully over a heat source, such as a light bulb or toaster, to make the writing appear.

....

398 Potato Prints

Make your own gift wrap. You will need a roll of plain white shelf paper, potatoes, and different-colored inkpads or tempera paint. Cut a potato in half, then carve out the design you want. Remember that the design will be the raised portion of the cutout. Stamp the potato first on the inkpad and then the paper.

399 Gingerbread Men

You Need: ★ ½ cup shortening ★ 1 egg ★ ½ cup brown sugar ★ 1½ cups flour ★ 1 package instant butterscotch pudding mix ★ 1½ tsp ginger ★ ½ tsp cinnamon ★ ½ tsp baking soda ★ Favorite frosting ★ Raisins and candies ★ Cookie cutter

Preheat the oven to 350°F. Mix together the egg, shortening, and brown sugar. Add the remaining ingredients to make a dough. Roll out the dough and cut into gingerbread men shapes with a cookie cutter. Bake for 10 minutes.

Decorate the men using favorite frosting, raisins, and candies. It's fun to make these after reading the classic tale of "The Gingerbread Man."

400 Freezer Jam

You Need: ★ 3 cups berries (raspberries, strawberries, or blueberries) ★ 3 cups sugar ★ Pectin

Have two or three plastic containers washed and at the ready. Have your child mush the berries in a bowl with the sugar. Dissolve the pectin according to the package instructions and pour into the berry mixture. After the mixture is well combined, pour into the clean containers and freeze or refrigerate.

You can eat the jam as soon as it cools, or it will keep in the freezer for up to six months.

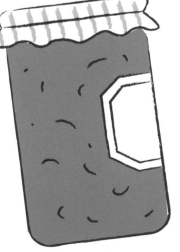

401 Peanut Butter

Peanut butter is super simple and very fun to make. It usually surprises kids that you can have your own peanut butter by simply grinding up peanuts, and it helps them develop a taste for the unsweetened kind.

Just take a few cups of shelled peanuts (salted or unsalted) and place them in a blender or food processor until the butter is a consistency you like. Peanuts have their own oil, so you shouldn't need to add any, but if your blender has trouble getting going, add a tablespoon of vegetable oil to "grease the wheels!"

402 Jam Pennies

You Need: ★ 12 slices of white or brown bread, crusts removed ★ 2 tbsp butter, softened ★ 6 oz strawberry jam

Make six jam sandwiches. Using a round pastry cutter, stamp out four circles from each sandwich. Arrange them on a serving plate and serve as soon as possible.

....

403 Food Foragers

Ask a local nature center or gardener what edible plants you could find in your area. If your lawn is chemical free, you could harvest the dandelion greens and wild strawberries in your own backyard, which are great in a salad. Look for watercress, or learn about various mushrooms that you can eat.

404 Blossoming Lunch

Daylilies bloom in July and August. This Asian-style recipe makes them totally yummy.

You Need: ★ 1-inch piece of ginger root, peeled and grated ★ 3 tbsp corn oil ★ 1 small can water chestnuts ★ 2–3 cups daylily buds ★ 1 tbsp soy sauce ★ 1 tsp sugar ★ 1 tbsp cornstarch ★ 3 tbsp water

Mix the sugar, cornstarch, soy sauce, and water and set aside. Heat the oil, add the ginger, and sauté for about 30 seconds. Add the water chestnuts and the daylily buds, and stir-fry. Pour the mixture over the lily buds, and turn quickly but gently until all the buds are coated with sauce. Serve immediately with rice or as a side dish.

405 Name the Card

A great way to keep a child busy before dinner, while enhancing their writing skills, is to have them make place cards for everyone.

Help your child decide how big he wants the place cards to be. Mark twice that size on some card and cut it out. Fold the card in half. Punch a hole in the corners nearest the fold. Now your child can write a name on one side of the card. Then decorate it with stickers or use crayons to draw around it.

Choose a color of yarn that looks best with the design, and tie it through the hole in the card for extra decoration.

406 Broccoli Apple Salad

You Need: ★ 4 apples ★ 1 tbsp lemon juice ★ 1 lb broccoli, cut into flowerets ★ ½ cup finely chopped red onion ★ ½ cup diced sweet red pepper ★ 1 cup garbanzo beans ★ ¼ cup of honey mustard salad dressing

Steam the broccoli for about 5 minutes until it is tender, and drain it in a colander. Run cold water over it to stop it from cooking any more.

Cut the apples into ³/₄-inch cubes and sprinkle with lemon juice. Toss to mix. Add the broccoli, red pepper and onion. Toss again. Add the beans and the salad dressing, and toss once more.

407 Dredging

To "dredge" or "bread" means to coat something lightly, usually using flour, cornmeal, or breadcrumbs. It creates a delicious crunchy, browned surface on foods that will be sautéed or fried.

Set out three bowls. Put some flour in one, some whipped egg in the second, and some cornmeal or breadcrumbs in the third bowl. Add some seasoning to the breadcrumbs to add flavor as well as crunch.

Sit your child in front of the bowls and ask him to dip each piece of fish or meat first in the flour, then in the egg, and finally into the cornmeal or breadcrumbs.

408 Dump Cake

You Need: ★ 1 can cherry pie filling ★ 1 x 20-oz can crushed pineapple with juice ★ 1 yellow cake mix ★ 1 x 8-oz bag chopped walnuts or pecans ★ 1 x 7-oz bag flaked or shredded coconut ★ ¼ cup butter, melted

Preheat oven to 350°F. Put the cherry pie filling and the pineapple with juice into a 13 x 9-inch baking pan. Spread around to combine the fruit a little. Sprinkle the dry cake mix evenly over the fruit. Sprinkle the nuts and coconut over the cake mix. Drizzle the butter evenly over the nuts and coconut. Bake for 40–50 minutes, or until the coconut looks toasty.

When the cake is cool, serve with ice cream.

409 Chocolate Spots

You Need: ★ Vanilla wafer cookies ★ Round pretzels ★ Candy hearts ★ Chocolate candies

Place the vanilla wafer cookies 1 inch apart on an ungreased cookie sheet. Set a chocolate candy on the center of each cookie. Bake at 200°F for 5 minutes. Remove from oven and gently press a candy heart into the center of the softened chocolate candy.

Now repeat the above using the pretzels instead of the wafer cookies. When you take them out of the oven and add the candy heart to the chocolate, you may need to wiggle the chocolate around a little to fill in any gaps between the chocolate and the pretzel.

410 My Kitchen Tools

Give your child her very own set of measuring cups and spoons, the more brightly colored the better. Then you can ask questions like *"Please pass me the blue cup,"* or *"Use the yellow spoon to stir it."*

411 Mini Meals

If you are making a family-sized meal, let your child spoon some of the mixture into a tiny baking dish, just for himself. Buy a miniature muffin pan so your child can make little baby muffins, or pick up a mini loaf pan to bake a kid-sized banana bread. Tiny food is more fun to make and eat.

412 Mash the Smash

Boil some potatoes so they are nice and soft. Add a little butter. Now choose your masher—a potato ricer for extra-smooth mash, or a potato masher for mash with a little more texture. Show your child how to use both and let them mash the smash!

413 Sweet Mashes

Mashing is not just for potatoes—there are loads of fruit desserts you can make that start with a mush. Slowly cook some apples in a tablespoon of water. Add some berries, peaches, or pears, and mash or purée depending on how smooth you like it.

414 Easy Appetizers

Spear cubes of cheese, cherry tomatoes, or chunks of ham on a bamboo skewer (be careful of little fingers). Arrange them on a plate with a puddle of dipping sauce (try Dijon mustard and mayonnaise, or creamy Italian dressing) and voilà—appetizers are served!

415 "Sushi" Rolls

You Need: ★ Cream cheese ★ 2 slices of cold cuts ★ 1 whole wheat wrap ★ Butter knife ★ Cutting board

Place the wrap on the cutting board. Spread cream cheese on the wrap, then add the cold cuts. Roll the stuffed wrap into a tight roll. Cut the roll into 8–10 pieces (each piece should be about 2 inches wide).

416 Personal Pizza

You Need: ★ 1 whole wheat pita ★ Cheese slices
★ Cherry tomatoes or tomato slices

Open the pita lengthwise. Place the cheese and tomatoes inside the pita. Put it in a microwave and cook for 30 seconds. Cut the "pizza" into 4 slices and serve.

417 Cinnamon Toast

You Need: ★ 2 slices of bread ★ Butter knife
★ Butter ★ Cinnamon

Put the bread in the toaster and toast until brown. While the toast is still warm, spread it with butter. Sprinkle cinnamon on top, and eat immediately—simple!

418 Homemade Parfait

You Need: ★ Vanilla yogurt ★ Mixed fruit (strawberries, bananas, and berries) ★ Honey

Half-fill a glass with yogurt. Top with mixed fruit. Drizzle honey on top and mix everything together.

419 Three-minute Cookies

You Need: ★ 2 cups granulated sugar ★ 8 tbsp butter ★ ½ cup low-fat milk ★ ⅓ cup baking cocoa ★ 3 cups oats

Mix the sugar, butter, milk, and cocoa in a pan. Bring to a boil over a medium heat for 3 minutes, stirring frequently. Remove from the heat. Stir in the oats. Drop tablespoonfuls on to waxed paper. Let stand until firm.

420 Apple Smiles

You Need: ★ 1 or more apples ★ Peanut butter
★ Mini marshmallows

Cut the apple into wedges. Spread peanut butter on one side of each wedge. Place 4 mini marshmallows on the peanut butter of one wedge, and another wedge on top!

421 Baggie Fudge

You Need: ★ ⅔ cup powder sugar ★ 1 tbsp margarine
★ ½ oz cream cheese ★ 1½ tbsp cocoa

Put all the ingredients into a ziplock sandwich bag. Allow your child to squish the mixture with their hands. It will soon mix up into a delicious fudge dip for wafers.

422 Crispy Cookies

You Need: ★ ½ cup light corn syrup ★ ½ cup peanut butter ★ 3 cups crisped rice

Moisten your child's hands first to stop them sticking. Mix all the ingredients together and shape into balls.

423 Rice Jam

Fill a jar with rice. Put the handle of a wooden spoon into the jar, wiggle it gently, then take it out. Then do it again. As you jiggle the handle, you should notice that the level of the rice drops and you will have to keep topping up the jar with rice. At some point you will find that it gets harder to move the handle. Eventually when you try and take the handle out, it stays stuck in the jar.

424 Monkey Bread

You Need: ★ ⅓ cup butter ★ 10-oz package of refrigerated buttermilk cookies, cut in half ★ ⅔ cup sugar ★ 1 tsp cinnamon

Microwave the butter for up to a minute in a small dish. Mix the sugar and cinnamon together in another dish. Roll each biscuit in the butter, then in the cinnamon mixture. Place each biscuit on its side around the outside of a pie plate. Microwave on 70 percent power for 5–7 minutes until the biscuits feel light and springy. Stand for 3–4 minutes. Turn upside down on a serving plate.

425 Eggshell Magic

Set a raw egg in a glass of white vinegar (acetic acid), so that it's completely covered in the liquid. Bubbles should start to form on the surface of the egg almost immediately. Let it sit for a week and then carefully take the egg out. The eggshell should have disappeared!

426 Racing Jam Jars

Make a racetrack by leaning a board against a chair. Collect three identical plastic jars. Keep one empty, fill one with water, and fill the third one with jam. Screw the lids on tightly. Race the three jars against one another in different combinations. Before the start of each race, guess to see which one will win.

427 Sugar Crystals

Use sugar and water to grow edible crystals!

Put ¾ cup of water in a small saucepan. Heat to boiling (don't let the kids do this on their own), then add 1½ cups of sugar, stirring until no more can be dissolved. Continue to heat the solution until it is clear. Pour the solution into a glass. Dip a piece of cotton into the solution so that the lower part of the cotton is coated. Take the string out and let it dry, then suspend it in the solution by tying one end to a pencil and setting the pencil over the glass.

Leave it for a week and see your crystals grow!

428 Salt Crystals

Fill two 6–8-oz cups with warm water and stir. Pour Epsom salt into each cup until no more salt will dissolve.

Tie a washer or other small weight to each end of a 12-inch piece of cotton. Set each end of the cotton in one of the cups, with the middle of the cotton hanging down loosely in a U shape. Set a plate underneath to catch the drips as the water and salt solution moves along to the middle of the string. After a few days, tiny crystals should form along the string.

429 What Smells?

Find four plastic film canisters. Punch a hole in each lid.
Put a strong-smelling object in each canister, such as
spices, citrus peel, toothpaste, and pencil shavings.
Have your children guess what's in each one.

430 Magnetic Cereal

Crush some breakfast cereal up into a powder. Put a
magnet into it and shake it around. Take the magnet out
and you should find that some of the cereal is sticking
to the magnet. If you have another, stronger magnet,
the cereal particles should jump across to the stronger
magnet when you bring them together.

431 Slush in a Flash

In this cool experiment you can freeze a bottle of lemonade right in front of your eyes!

Add some water to a large bowl of ice so the ice is about half-covered in water. Add several tablespoons of salt to the ice. Bury a small bottle of unopened fizzy drink in the ice and wait for 20–30 minutes (if the drink freezes you have waited too long).

Open the bottle. The bottle should turn to slush in a few seconds in front of your eyes.

Cool!

432 Rainbow Cake

You Need: ★ 1 package vanilla cake mix ★ Food coloring (three different colors)

Prepare the cake mix according to the instructions on the package. Divide the mixture into three bowls. Add a few drops of different food coloring to each bowl and let your toddler mix the colors in.

When your toddler has finished mixing, let him spoon the mixture into a greased cake pan in any sequence he likes. He'll be delighted by the muddle of colors they are creating. Bake the cake as per the package instructions.

433 Summer Muesli

You Need: ★ 1 cup dried apples ★ ½ cup of dried coconut ★ 1 cup dried apricots ★ ½ cup sliced almonds ★ ½ cup of dried mango ★ ½ cup dried cranberries ★ 1 cup raisins ★ ½ cup of sunflower seeds ★ 2 cups rolled oats ★ Honey (optional)

Cut the dried apples, apricots, mangoes, and cranberries into small pieces, and put all the chopped fruit in a large bowl. Combine with the remaining ingredients. Mix them together gently.

Serve with yogurt and a teaspoon of honey.

434 Tropical Smoothie

You Need: ★ 1 mango ★ 1 banana ★ 1 cup pineapple juice ★ 1 cup of coconut milk (unsweetened) ★ 1 cup plain sweetened yogurt ★ 1 cup of ice

Peel and chop the fruit into cubes. Place the ingredients all together in a blender and blend until smooth. Pour into tall glasses and serve.

435 Fruit Smoothie

You Need: ★ 1 cup frozen mixed berries ★ 2 bananas ★ 1 cup of soy milk ★ ½ cup vanilla ice cream

Peel and chop the banana into cubes. Place all the ingredients into a blender and blend until smooth. Pour into tall glasses and serve.

436 Holes Game

Take a big piece of posterboard and cut some holes in it, big enough to put your head or hands through. Tape one edge to a wall, so that the board sticks out into the room.

Let your toddler stand on one side and you sit on the other. Have her put some objects through the holes and let you pass them back. She can stick her hand through and you can tickle it or grab it. Pass stuffed animals through, and toss them over. Describe the objects before you pass them back.

437 Hands and Feet

Cut out some felt handprints and footprints of many different colors. Put them on the floor and have your toddler jump on the footprints and put his hands down on the handprints. Your toddler will love to jump around the room and the game can be used to learn colors.

438 Puzzle Flashlight Hunt

Take the pieces from one of your favorite puzzles and hide them in a room that you can darken. Take a walk with your toddler and a flashlight and try to find all the pieces of the puzzle. As you find each one, try to put it in the right place in the puzzle.

439 Window Wash

Take some clear contact paper and fold it in half to the size of about 8 x 11 inches (sticky sides together). Use a permanent marker and draw the outline of a window on one side. On the other side, wet the contact paper and sprinkle on some cinnamon. This will be the "dirt" that your toddler will wipe off.

Tape the "window" to a real window or to a piece of cardboard with a picture on it. Then let your toddler use a damp washcloth or paper towel and wipe off the dirt to see what is on the other side of the window!

440 Giant's Paintbrush

You Need: ★ Empty water bottle ★ Dishwashing sponge ★ Rubber band ★ Washable paints

Take an empty water bottle with the cap still on and peel off the label. Cut a strip off a dish sponge and wrap it over the top. Secure it with a rubber band. Put some non-toxic washable paints on a plate and let your toddler hold the bottle with the sponge down and dip it into the paints.

Use the giant's brush to paint on large sheets of paper. Try different techniques like stamping and sweeping.

441 Ice Bath

Freeze a small bath toy in a plastic cup of water. When your toddler is having a bath, remove the frozen toy from the cup and watch the ice melt in the bath. The toy will be released into the bath!

442 Shaker Art

Purchase containers of salt, peppercorns, and colored spices, such as dried ginger. Pour into clean, dry spice shakers. Then, give your child a glue stick and some stiff paper or a paper plate. Encourage her to scribble all over the paper with the glue. Then give your child the shakers and have her shake it onto the glue. Show her how to shake off the excess, leaving the remaining art.

443 Crayon Squares

Toddlers love to drop things, so why
not make a game of it? Take a piece of
paper and draw a line down the middle
lengthwise and a line across widthwise to
make four rectangle boxes of equal size.
Write the name of each player in a box, or
get them to write or draw their own marker.

Have your toddler hold about five crayons above the
paper and drop them. See which ones land in which box.
Count the tips of the crayons in each box and give
a point for each. Keep score by writing in the boxes.

444 Go Fish

Put a number of small bath toys in the water and give your child a net to catch them with. Shout out the name of a toy and see how quickly she can catch it.

445 Five Ball Kicker

Take five balls of different sizes and colors. Place them in a line on the ground and have your toddler kick each one (or throw it). Count each one as your toddler kicks it. He will want to do it over and over.

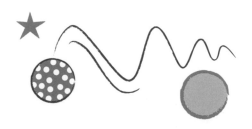

446 Musical Color

This is a variation on musical chairs. Give your toddler, yourself, and any other kids a sheet of paper and start the music. Everyone colors their sheet with a crayon until the music stops. Then the sheets of paper are all passed on to your neighbor. The music starts up, and everyone starts coloring again. When the music stops, pass the papers on again!

At the end you'll all have a piece of paper that everyone has drawn on and shared the coloring activity with. Put the artwork on display for everyone to see.

447 Cereal Sidewalk

Cut open a bunch of empty cereal boxes and cut off the top and bottom flaps. Lay them down on the floor in a line and let your toddler crawl, toddle, or walk over them. Talk about what color she sees, what color her foot is on, or what object she is standing on.

448 Toddler Decorator

Cut out felt circles and strips of all different colors, then let your toddler "decorate." Take a circle with tape on it and put it on the drapes to give polka dots. Take strips of paper and put them on the couch to make plaid or striped patterns. Remember to take a photograph.

449 Block Truck

Take an empty oatmeal container and gather together some of your toddler's blocks. Cut a square in the container's lid that will allow a block to fit through. Cut a rectangle about double the size of the opening in the lid on the side of the container.

Have your toddler start to put blocks in the opening on the lid. When she has put in a few, let her roll the container slowly along the floor and see the blocks fall out through the side opening. Let her do it again and again—as many times as she would like.

450 Night Light Clothes

Spread out different articles of your toddler's clothing on the floor. Turn on a flashlight and place it inside one piece of clothing.

Turn off the lights and ask your toddler to find the flashlight. Ask if it is under the shirt? Or in the sock? After he finds it, let him put it in something and ask you to look for it! You can also play with two flashlights and two of each article of clothing. Then you put the flashlight in a sock and ask your toddler to do the same thing. Then turn off the lights and ask where the flashlights are.

451 Blanket Balance

Take all of those old receiving blankets and roll or fold them up to make a line on the carpet. Hold your toddler's hand and help her walk along the "balance beam" of rolled blankets. See if she can jump on the beam or walk backwards along the beam.

452 Tracing Shapes Hunt

Cut out a circle, square, and triangle from a large piece of cardboard. Give your toddler a large sheet of paper on which to make a picture or design by tracing then coloring the shapes. Write his name at the top of the picture, spelling it out letter by letter as you write.

453 Animal Safari

Ask your youngster to look for and cut out pictures of animals from old magazines. Help him glue or paste the pictures on a large sheet of paper. Then ask him to name as many of the animals as he can. Write each animal name under the picture and spell out the letters as you write.

454 Sandpaper Play

Give your child a piece of sandpaper and some wood scraps. Show her how to sand the wood, and talk about the difference between rough and smooth textures. The wood can be glued together to create sculptures. To avoid splinters, you may want your child to wear gloves.

455 Bean Game

Take an amount of beans or counters to hold in your
hands. Decide on a number, for example eight, to work
on. Have your toddler count out eight beans. Place the
beans in your hands and hide them behind your back.
Divide them between your hands—for example three in
one hand and five in the other. Show the beans in one
hand. Your toddler must tell you how many you have in
the other hand. Play again using different combinations.

You can also turn this educational game into a simple
but fun guessing game.

One, two, three, four...

456 Writing Cream

Lay out waxed paper or tinfoil on a work counter or kitchen table. Let the kids spray a large pile of shaving cream onto the area. Have them spread out the cream then practice their writing skills in it. Use this fun, messy activity to practice writing letters, words, and numbers.

457 Coin Hit

You need a quarter and a playground ball for this outdoor activity. The players stand behind their own sidewalk section facing each other and place a quarter standing upright in the sidewalk crack between them.

The first player stands behind the line of their sidewalk section and tries to hit the standing quarter by bouncing the ball at it. If he hits the quarter, he gets one point and if it is knocked out of the crack he gets two points. Then it's the second player's turn. The first player to 21 points is the winner.

458 Crayon Treasure

Buy three or four large boxes of crayons and hide the crayons throughout your playing area. Give all the players bags to collect the crayons, and send them off searching for the colorful crayon treasure.

When the treasure hunt is over, the player with the most crayons gets to keep the box that they came in. Players can also go around trading different colors with each other.

459 Backyard Volcano

You Need: ★ A baking pan ★ Soda bottle (16 or 20 oz) ★ Moist soil ★ Baking soda ★ Vinegar ★ Red food coloring

Place the baking pan on the grass and set the soda bottle in the middle. Pile up and shape the moist soil around the bottle to form a volcano. Bring the soil right up to the top of the bottle's opening, but don't get any inside the bottle. Pour one tablespoon of baking soda into the bottle. Color one cup of vinegar with red food coloring. Pour the vinegar into the bottle. Stand back a safe distance and watch red lava spray out of the top your backyard volcano.

460 Crystal Creator

You Need: ★ Water ★ Alum (sold in the spice or canning sections of supermarkets) ★ Clear glass bowl ★ Rocks and pebbles ★ Mixing spoon

Your child should go outside and gather as many rocks and pebbles as she likes. Rinse the rocks clean in the sink or tub. On the stove, boil half a cup of water. Add 2 oz alum to the hot water and stir until the alum is dissolved. Pour the solution into a clear glass bowl. Fill the bowl halfway with the clean rocks and pebbles. Now watch in amazement as crystals form like magic!

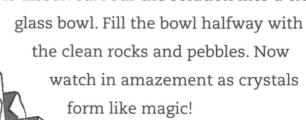

461 Chalk Rub

Send your toddlers out with chalk and paper to look for different textures. Have them put several small samples on a large piece of paper by placing the paper on the object and rubbing across it with the chalk. Suggest that they try trees, the sidewalk, patio bricks, corrugated lawn furniture, and tile flooring.

Make sure they know not to go off the paper, which could cause damage to the house or other materials. After they are done, ask them what they have found.

462 Cereal Necklace

Cut one piece of string about 20–26 inches long for each child. Put a piece of transparent tape on one end of the string. Supply a variety of ring-shaped cereal pieces. Have your toddlers string on the cereal in the pattern of their choice. You can attach the ends of their necklace with transparent tape—which if pulled would come apart quickly. Always monitor where and how long your child wears anything around his neck.

After making the necklace, the great part is eating the cereal off the string!

463 Junk Mail

Save up all your junk mail for this activity. Use a shoebox and cut one end so that it opens like a real mailbox after you've taped the lid to the box.

Write your toddler's name and address down on a piece of paper. Have her practice writing her name on unwanted junk mail forms. On blank envelopes she can learn how to address mail. For little ones, give them old address labels to stick on. When older children have mastered writing and addressing envelopes, have them write to someone they know. They can send a self-addressed stamped envelope with a piece of paper for the recipient to respond.

464 Lace Cards

Use old or unwanted greeting cards and punch holes around the outer edge of each one with a hole punch while the card is closed.

Take pieces of yarn and make one end usable for young fingers. You can do this by either placing a small drop of glue on the end of the string and letting it dry, or by placing a small piece of tape on the end of the string.

Have your toddlers weave string around the outer edge of the card for decoration. They can also use glue thinned out with water to cover the front of card before adding glitter.

465 Make a Fort

For a rainy day activity, nothing beats making a fort with blankets inside the house or basement. Use a few chairs, a small table, and some blankets and sheets. When it's finished, make sure you crawl in with your toddler to experience the fun of being little again!

466 Package Wrap

Find items for little ones to practice wrapping, such as a toy or several small boxes. Supply them with old wrapping paper or comics, and supply plenty of tape. Depending on age, either supply scissors or pre-cut paper. Decorate with bows, ribbons, string, and tags.

467 Picture Scavenger Hunt

Make a scavenger hunt list with pictures you have drawn on a sheet of paper. You could draw a feather, small stone, various leaf designs, small twig or stick, pinecone, flower (only if they are allowed to pick one), worm, piece of grass, clover leaf. Then let the hunt begin.

468 Popsicle Fan

Make a fan using popsicle sticks and thin cardboard backing, perhaps recycling the cardboard that comes out of the packages of pantyhose or using a paper plate.

Cut the cardboard into the desired fan shape. Help your toddlers color their fans with crayons. They can also glue on glitter and beads, or make holes with a hole punch. You could also string ribbon through the holes. Glue or staple the cardboard to the stick and fan away.

469 Popsicle Puppet

Ask your child to look through magazines for pictures of people and animals. Cut out the pictures and glue them to a piece of backing card. Cut the card to the same shape. Glue to a popsicle stick and come up with an idea for a play using the new popsicle puppets.

470 Popcorn Tambourine

Place a paper plate face up on the table. Pour in a tablespoon of popcorn seeds and place a second paper plate upside down on top. Staple around the edges. Decorate your tambourine with a hole punch between the staples. Color it, weave in pieces of ribbon, and tie on some small bells.

471 Pretend Painting

Give your toddlers a paintbrush and a can of water. Tell them to imagine the water is paint, and ask them to paint the house, garage, or fence. Ask them what color their paint is as they paint different things.

472 Rocks and Pebbles

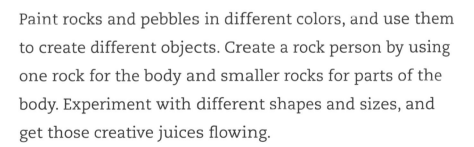

Paint rocks and pebbles in different colors, and use them to create different objects. Create a rock person by using one rock for the body and smaller rocks for parts of the body. Experiment with different shapes and sizes, and get those creative juices flowing.

473 For the Birds

Go outside and observe your local birds. Feed them different types of food—seeds, fruits, etc. Tell your preschoolers that they are now scientists and have them gather all types of data. Have them keep records and make charts of the types of food the birds prefer and the amount they consume in a day or a week. Have them note the consistency of feeding patterns and how they are affected by the weather. They can compare the number of birds feeding in the morning and afternoon.

They can also note the types of birds attracted by different foods and feeders. The list goes on! Have the children make posters and displays of their results.

Rhymes & Fingerplays

474 Rhyme Time

Ask your child to pick out the odd non-rhyming word from a list of rhyming words that you say out loud. For example, cat, sat, mat, pot, rat, hat. Clap your hands and keep rhythm as you play the game.

475 I-Spy Rhyme

Play "I spy" but use rhyming words as your clues. For example: "I spy with my little eye something that rhymes with hat." Then your toddler must guess that you are looking at a mat. You can have fun gathering together different pairs of objects that have rhyming names.

476 Fill the Blank

Say a nursery rhyme that your child knows, but leave out the rhyming word and ask him to fill in the missing word. For example, you say, *"Hickory dickory dock, the mouse ran up the...."* Your toddler must say *"clock."*

477 Clap Handies

Clap hands together as you sing the following rhyme:

Clap handies, clap handies for Daddy to come
Daddy's got sweeties and Mommy's got none.

478 This Little Pig

Count out each pig on your toddler's fingers, starting with the little finger. When you reach the thumb, tickle your toddler instead!

This little pig went to market.
This little pig stayed at home.
This little pig had roast beef.
This little pig had none
And this little pig cried: "Wee! wee!"
All the way home.

479 This Little Mousie

Count out each little mouse on your toddler's toes, starting with the little toe. Repeat the rhyme for the other foot, and teach your toddler the words. You can also use this rhyme to practice counting.

This little mousie peeped within
This little mousie walked right in!
This little mousie came to play,
This little mousie ran away!
This little mousie cried, "Dear me!
Dinner is done and it's time for tea!"

480 Round and Round

While singing this rhyme, circle your finger on the palm of your toddler's hand, walk your fingers up your toddler's arm, then tickle him under the armpit. Delighted laughter is assured every time!

Round and round the garden
Goes the teddy bear
One step, two steps
Tickle him under there.

481 Hokey Pokey

Everyone stands in a circle. Sing and do the actions:

You put your left foot in, you take your left foot out,
You put your left foot in and you shake it all about.
You do the Hokey Pokey and you turn around,
(now clap with each word) and that's what it's all about.

★ Repeat the tune with each foot, then each arm. You
  can end with putting your head in, your bottom, or
  your whole self!

482 Popcorn

Huddle in a ball, then jump up, then dance around:

I'm a little popcorn in a pot,
Heat me up and watch me pop!
When I am all white I'm done,
Popping corn is lots of fun!

483 Ring A Ring

Join hands and dance in a circle for this old favorite, then all fall down!

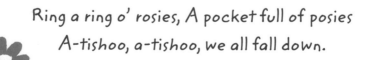

Ring a ring o' rosies, A pocket full of posies
A-tishoo, a-tishoo, we all fall down.

484 Incy, Wincy

Put the index finger of your right hand to the thumb of your left hand and the index finger of your left hand on the thumb of your right hand. Alternate to mimic the spider climbing up the water spout. Mimic rain falling from the sky and then whoosh your hands as the spider is "washed out." Put your hands in a circle to show the sun coming up. Then repeat as the spider climbs again.

Incy, wincy spider climbed the water spout.
Down came the rain and washed the spider out.
Out came the sunshine and dried up all the rain.
Incy, wincy spider climbed up the spout again.

485 Rock-A-Bye Baby

Pretend to rock a baby in your arms (or you can use a favorite doll or stuffed animal) while this rhyme is sung.

Rock-a-bye baby, on the tree top
When the wind blows, the cradle will rock
When the bough breaks, the cradle will fall
Down will come baby, cradle and all.

486 I'm A Little Teapot

The actions for this treasured rhyme are to put one hand on one hip and stick one hand out, so that you form your teapot shape. Then, of course, you and the kids tip yourselves up to pour your tea!

I'm a little teapot, short and stout
Here's my handle, here's my spout
When I see the teacups, hear me shout:
"Pick me up and pour me out!"

487 Teddy Bear

Act out the rhyme with your teddy bears!

Teddy bear, teddy bear, turn around
Teddy bear, teddy bear, touch the ground
Teddy bear, teddy bear, climb the stairs
Teddy bear, teddy bear, say your prayers
Teddy bear, teddy bear, turn out the light
Teddy bear, teddy bear, say "Good night!"

488 The Wheels on the Bus

Act out each verse of this song with your hands—it's
a great circle-time song! You can also make up verses.
Ask your kids what the daddies on the bus do—or the
windows, lights, or doors!

The wheels on the bus go round and round
Round and round, round and round
The wheels on the bus go round and round
All over town.
The moms on the bus go natter, natter, natter
etc… all over town.
The kids on the bus go wriggle, wriggle, wriggle
etc… all over town.
The grannies on the bus go knit, knit, knit
etc… all over town.

489 Row, Row, Row

Two people sit facing each other, with legs slightly bent in front of them and their feet touching each other. Hold each other's hands and rock forward and back in a rowing motion as you sing together:

> Row, row, row your boat
> Gently down the stream.
> Merrily, merrily, merrily, merrily,
> Life is but a dream!

490 This Is The Way

Your toddler should sit on your knees for this irresistible singing game. Bounce and rock your knees at different speeds and angles to imitate the different riders in the rhyme. You can do a soft flop to the floor at the end.

This is the way the ladies ride,
Nimble, nimble, nimble.
This is the way the gentlemen ride,
A gallop, a trot, a gallop, a trot.
This is the way the farmers ride,
Joggety-jog, joggety-jog.
And when they come to a hedge—they jump over!
And when they come to a slippery space—
They scramble, scramble, scramble,
Tumble down Dick!

491 Here We Go Round

Skip around your living room and act out the washing of the clothes for this old-timey rhyme!

Here we go round the mulberry bush,
The mulberry bush, the mulberry bush,
Here we go round the mulberry bush
On a cold and frosty morning.
This is the way we wash our clothes,
Wash our clothes, wash our clothes,
This is the way we wash our clothes,
On a cold and frosty morning.

492 The Grand Old Duke

This marching song has been keeping toddlers happy for many years. You'll have great fun watching your children march around the room, and then hearing them learn the rhyme:

The Grand old Duke of York,
He had ten thousand men,
He marched them up to the top of the hill
And he marched them down again.
When they were up, they were up,
And when they were down, they were down,
And when they were only halfway up
They were neither up nor down.

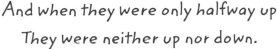

3+ 1+ 10 →

493 Five Little Speckled Frogs

This one goes just like it sounds. Put your fingers up for as many frogs as are left and pretend to eat the most delicious bugs! Rub your tummy—they're good.

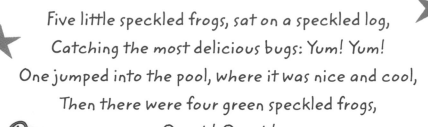

Five little speckled frogs, sat on a speckled log,
Catching the most delicious bugs: Yum! Yum!
One jumped into the pool, where it was nice and cool,
Then there were four green speckled frogs,
Quark! Quark!
Four little speckled frogs...
(REPEAT UNTIL THERE ARE NO
GREEN SPECKLED FROGS.)

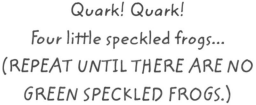

494 1-2-3-4-5

Count out on your fingers and pretend to be bitten at the end. You can switch fingers—or add other body parts, if you find your toddler wants to keep the rhyme going!

1-2-3-4-5, Once I caught a fish alive
6-7-8-9-10, Then I let him go again.
Why did you let him go?
Because he bit my finger so,
Which finger did he bite?
This little finger on my right.

495 Ten Green Bottles

Show your ten fingers and dwindle down to one—or as long your toddler is interested. This is a great song for learning to count backward!

Ten green bottles hanging on the wall
Ten green bottles hanging on the wall
And if one green bottle should accidentally fall
There'll be nine green bottles hanging on the wall.
Nine green bottles hanging on the wall…
(REPEAT UNTIL THERE ARE NO GREEN BOTTLES
HANGING ON THE WALL.)

496 One, Two, Buckle My Shoe

Just pretend to do each action as it comes up in the song. Pick up the sticks, lay them straight, and onward!

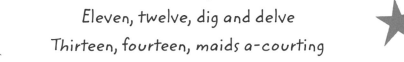

One, two, buckle my shoe
Three, four, knock at the door
Five, six, pick up sticks
Seven, eight, lay them straight
Nine, ten, a big fat hen
Eleven, twelve, dig and delve
Thirteen, fourteen, maids a-courting
Fifteen, sixteen, maids in the kitchen
Seventeen, eighteen, maids in waiting
Nineteen, twenty, my plate's empty.

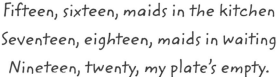

2+ | 1+ | 15 | →

497 The Farmer and the Dell

The Farmer and the Dell, The Farmer and the Dell,
Hi ho the derry-o, The Farmer and the Dell,
The Farmer takes a wife, The Farmer takes a wife,
Hi ho the derry-o, The Farmer takes a wife.

Sing and repeat, changing the last two lines for: The wife takes a child; The child takes a nurse; The nurse takes a dog; The dog takes a cat; The cat takes a mouse; The mouse takes the cheese; The cheese stands alone. Stand the children in a circle. One child in the middle is the farmer, who chooses a wife, and so on.

Marry me...

498 One, He Loves

This is a counting song to be sung as you pull the petals from a daisy. Stop when you run out of petals!

One he loves, two, he loves,
Three, he loves, they say.
Four he loves with all his heart;
Five he casts away.
Six he loves, seven she loves;
Eight they both love.
Nine, he comes; ten he tarries;
Eleven, he courts, twelve, he marries.

499 Five Rosy Apples

Try this with real apples or balls, placing them out in a row and having each child take a turn grabbing one away. It can easily be done on fingers, too!

Five rosy apples by the cottage door,
One tumbled off a twig
and then there were four.
Four rosy apples by the cottage door,
The farmer's wife took one and then there were three.
Three rosy apples by the cottage door,
I think I'll have one and then there'll be two.
Two rosy apples hanging in the sun,
You have the big one and that will leave one.
One rosy apple, soon it is gone.
The wind blew it off the branch
and now there are none.

500 Polly Put the Kettle On

This is just a sweet little rhyme to sing. You could also act it out with a real or pretend tea set.

Polly put the kettle on,
Polly put the kettle on,
Polly put the kettle on,
We'll all have tea.

Sukie take it off again,
Sukie take it off again,
Sukie take it off again,
They've all gone away.

Index

Author acknowledgments

Many thanks, as always, to my family—John, Matt, Lydia, Alex, Liam, Jack, and Kiara. I am also very grateful to the many parents and teachers who wrote to me—or just stopped me at a ball game—and said, "Here's a great activity for you..." And to Caroline Earle and Jason Hook who kept me on track during the process.